I0439034

Coordinated Bird Monitoring: Technical Recommendations for Military Lands

By Jonathan Bart and Ann Manning, U.S. Geological Survey; Leah Dunn, Great Basin Bird Observatory; Richard Fischer and Chris Eberly, Department of Defense Partners in Flight

Prepared in cooperation with the DoD Natural Resources Program, Arlington, Virginia; Great Basin Bird Observatory, Reno, Nevada; U.S. Army Engineer Research and Development Center, Environmental Laboratory, Vicksburg, Mississippi; DoD Partners in Flight, Warrenton, Virginia

**A Report Prepared for the Department of Defense Legacy Resource Management Program
Legacy Project # 05-246, 06-246, 07-246**

Open-File Report 2010–1078

**U.S. Department of the Interior
U.S. Geological Survey**

U.S. Department of the Interior
KEN SALAZAR, Secretary

U.S. Geological Survey
Marcia K. McNutt, Director

U.S. Geological Survey, Reston, Virginia: 2012

For more information on the USGS—the Federal source for science about the Earth, its natural and living resources, natural hazards, and the environment, visit http://www.usgs.gov or call 1-888-ASK-USGS.

For an overview of USGS information products, including maps, imagery, and publications, visit *http://www.usgs.gov/pubprod*

To order this and other USGS information products, visit *http://store.usgs.gov*

The DoD Legacy Resource Management Program funded this project. For more information, visit *https://www.dodlegacy.org*

For more information on the DoD Natural Resources Conservation Program, visit http://www.dodnaturalresources.net. For more information on the DoD Partners in Flight Program, visit http://www.dodpif.orgSuggested citation:
Bart, J., Manning, A., Dunn, L., Fischer, R., and Eberly, C., 2012, Coordinated bird monitoring: Technical recommendations for military lands: U.S. Geological Survey Open-File Report 2010-1078, 68 p.

Any use of trade, product, or firm names is for descriptive purposes only and does not imply endorsement by the U.S. Government.

Although this report is in the public domain, permission must be secured from the individual copyright owners to reproduce any copyrighted material contained within this report.

Contents

Executive Summary.. 1

Chapter 1: Project Summary... 4
Chapter 2: Review of DoD's Existing Bird Monitoring Programs... 14
Chapter 3. Emerging Technologies for Monitoring... 16
Chapter 4: Guidelines for Designing Short-Term Bird Monitoring Programs.............................. 24
Chapter 5: Selecting a Survey Method 33
Chapter 6: Data Management.. 36
Chapter 7: Recommendations for Surveying Species of Concern 40
Chapter 8: Recommendations for Participation in Large-Scale Surveys..................................... 44
Chapter 9: Implementation... 48

Acknowledgments.. 49
References Cited 49
Appendix A. List of Avian Studies at DoD Installations 52

Figures

Figure 1. Estimates of the number of surveys needed for CV=0.2 based on surveys of piping plovers (PIPL, *Charadrius melodus*) and snowy plovers (SNPL, *C. alexandrinus*) in Florida during October–March. 31
Figure 2. Data management in the DoD CBM program. 39

Tables

Table 1. Goals and recommendations in the U.S. NABCI report, "Opportunities for improving avian monitoring"..... 5
Table 2. Selected passages from the MOU between DoD and the U.S. Fish and Wildlife Service to promote the conservation of migratory birds.. 6
Table 3. Selected passages from the Final Rule by the USFWS pertaining to "take of migratory birds by the Armed Forces" 7
Table 4. Ten steps to successful bird conservation through improved monitoring 8
Table 5. Types of bird monitoring and assessment projects on DoD lands, including projects completed during the last 10 years 15
Table 6. Outline used to describe short-term bird monitoring projects... 24
Table 7. Survey methods and required assumptions 35
Table 8. Recommendations to the Department of Defense (DoD) for management of historic records, inventory, and new monitoring projects 37
Table 9. Number of DoD properties with significant concentrations of migratory birds for at least a part of the year and numbers of properties known to contain at least one Species of Concern (SOC)............................ 41
Table 10. Number of Breeding Bird Survey (BBS) routes classified by distance to a DoD installation and recent survey frequency 44
Table 11. Current DoD-MAPS monitoring objectives relating to Readiness and Range Sustainment identifying DoD locations (number of MAPS stations) and target species (including two USFWS Focal Species—Wood Thrush and Painted Bunting)... 47

Conversion Factors

Multiply	By	To obtain
Mass		
gram (g)	0.03527	ounce, avoirdupois (oz)
Length		
centimeter (cm)	0.3937	inch (in.)
millimeter (mm)	0.03937	inch (in.)
meter (m)	3.281	foot (ft)
kilometer (km)	0.6214	mile (mi)
kilometer (km)	0.5400	mile, nautical (nmi)
meter (m)	1.094	yard (yd)

Abbreviations and Acronyms

AAL	above antenna level
ABC	American Bird Conservancy
APA	Administrative Procedures Act
AKN	Avian Knowledge Network
ARU	autonomous recording units
BASH	Bird/Animal Aircraft Strike Hazard
BBIRD	Breeding Bird Research and Monitoring Database
BBS	North American Breeding Bird Survey
BMDE	Bird Monitoring Data Exchange
CBC	Christmas Bird Count
CBM	Coordinated Bird Monitoring
CBMD	Coordinated Bird Monitoring Database
CI	confidence interval
CV	coefficient of variation
DoD	Department of Defense
DoD PIF	DoD Partners in Flight
FOIA	Freedom of Information Act
FRESC	Forest and Rangeland Ecosystems Science Center
GBIF	Global Biodiversity Information Facility
GPS	Global Positioning System
IBP	The Institute for Bird Populations
INRMP	Integrated Natural Resources Management Plan
Legacy	DoD Legacy Resource Management Program

Abbreviations and Acronyms—Continued

MAPS	Monitoring Avian Productivity and Survivorship
MAWS	Monitoring Avian Winter Survival
MBTA	Migratory Bird Treaty Act
MoSI	Monitoreo de Sobrevivencia Invernal
MOU	Memorandum of Understanding
NABCI	North American Bird Conservation Initiative
NBII	USGS National Biological Information Infrastructure program
NE CBM Plan	Northeast Coordinated Bird Monitoring Plan
NEPA	National Environmental Policy Act
NEXRAD	NEXt generation RADar
NOAA	National Oceanic and Atmospheric Administration
NRMP	Natural Resources Monitoring Partnership
NWS	National Weather Service
PIF	Partners in Flight
PRISM	Program for Regional and International Shorebird Monitoring
RF	radio frequency
SE	standard error
SERDP	Strategic Environmental Research and Development Program
SOC	species of concern
USDA	U.S. Department of Agriculture
USFWS	U.S. Fish and Wildlife Service
USGS	U.S. Geological Survey
WSR-88D	Weather Surveillance Radar, 1988-Doppler

Coordinated Bird Monitoring: Technical Recommendations for Military Lands

By Jonathan Bart and Ann Manning, U.S. Geological Survey; Leah Dunn, Great Basin Bird Observatory; Richard Fischer and Chris Eberly, Department of Defense Partners in Flight

Executive Summary

The Department of Defense (DoD) is subject to several rules and regulations establishing responsibilities for monitoring migratory birds. The Sikes Act requires all military installations with significant natural resources to prepare and implement Integrated Natural Resources Management Plans (INRMPs). These plans guide the conservation and long-term management of natural resources on military lands in a manner that is compatible with and sustains the military mission. An INRMP also supports compliance with all legal requirements and guides the military in fulfilling its obligation to be a good steward of public land.

The management and conservation of migratory birds is addressed in installation INRMPs. The National Environmental Policy Act (NEPA) requires federal agencies to evaluate and disclose the potential environmental impacts of their proposed actions. More recently, DoD signed an MOU (*http://www.dodpif.org/downloads/EO13186_MOU-DoD.pdf*) for migratory birds, under Executive Order 13186, with the US Fish and Wildlife Service (USFWS) in July 2006 and a Migratory Bird Rule (*http://www.dodpif.org/downloads/MigBirdFINALRule_FRFeb2007.pdf*) was passed by Congress in February 2007. The Migratory Bird Rule addresses the potential impacts of military readiness activities on populations of migratory birds and establishes a process to implement conservation measures if and when a military readiness activity is expected to have a significant adverse impact on a population of migratory bird species (as determined through the NEPA process). The MOU states that for non-military readiness activities, prior to initiating any activity likely to affect populations of migratory birds DoD shall (1) identify the migratory bird species likely to occur in the area of the proposed action and determine if any species of concern could be affected by the activity, and (2) assess and document, using NEPA when applicable, the effect of the proposed action on species of concern. By following these procedures, DoD will minimize the possibility for a proposed action to unintentionally take migratory birds at a level that would violate any of the migratory bird treaties and potentially impact mission activities. In addition, implementing conservation and monitoring programs for migratory birds supports the ecosystem integrity necessary to sustain DoD's natural resources for the military mission.

Non-compliance with the procedural requirements of the MBTA could result in a private party lawsuit under the Administrative Procedures Act (APA). A lawsuit filed under APA involving a Navy bombing range is the basis for a court ruling that unintentional take of migratory birds applies to federal actions. Ensuring the necessary data is available to adequately assess impacts of a proposed action will help avoid lawsuits or help ensure such lawsuits have no grounds. The data gathered in a bird monitoring program will provide the best scientific data available to assess the expected impacts of a proposed action on migratory bird species through the NEPA process.

This report presents recommendations developed by the U.S. Geological Survey (USGS) for the Department of Defense (DoD) on establishing a "Coordinated Bird Monitoring (CBM) Plan." The CBM Plan is intended to ensure that DoD meets its conservation and regulatory responsibilities for monitoring birds (Chapter 1). The report relies heavily on recommendations in the report, "Opportunities for improving avian monitoring" (*http://www.nabci-us.org/aboutnabci/monitoringreportfinal0307.pdf*), by the U.S. North American Bird Conservation Initiative (U.S. NABCI Monitoring Subcommittee, 2007) and on a review of 358 current DoD bird monitoring programs carried out as part of this project (Chapter 2).

This report contains 12 recommendations which, if followed, would result in a comprehensive, efficient, and useful approach to bird monitoring. The recommendations are based on the entire report but are presented together at the end of Chapter 1. DoD has agreed to consider implementing these recommendations; however, final decisions will be based upon such factors as the availability of resources and military mission considerations. These recommendations from USGS can be summarized into 6 major themes:

1. A major report on monitoring was released in 2007 by the U.S. North American Bird Conservation Initiative (*http://www.nabci-us.org/main2.html*). DoD can be consistent with this report by establishing policy that monitoring will be explicitly acknowledged as an integral element of bird management and conservation (Recommendation 1).

2. The design of monitoring and assessment programs for birds should include the following steps:

   a. Preparation of a document describing the program's goals, objectives, and methods similar to a format we provide (Recommendation 2, Chapter 4).

   b. Selection of field methods using an "expert system" developed in this project (Recommendation 3, Chapter 5) or another well-documented system.

   c. Preparation and storage of metadata describing the monitoring program in the Natural Resources Monitoring Partnership (NRMP), and other appropriate databases (Recommendation 4, Chapter 6).

   d. Entry of the survey data using eBird (*http://ebird.org/content/dod*) or the Coordinated Bird Monitoring Database (CBMD) and long-term storage of the data in the CBMD and the Avian Knowledge Network (AKN; Recommendation 5, Chapter 6; *http://www.avianknowledge.net/*).

   e. Submission of major results from the monitoring program for publication in a peer-reviewed journal (Recommendation 6).

3. The DoD Legacy Resource Management Program (Legacy; *https://www.dodlegacy.org*), Environmental Security Technology Certification Program (ESTCP; *http://www.serdp.org/*), and Strategic Environmental Research and Development Program (SERDP; *http://www.serdp.org/*) should be encouraged to continue their significant contributions to the foundations of bird monitoring (Recommendation 7, Chapters 1 and 3).

4. Appropriate monitoring should be conducted to identify species of concern on installations. A year-round, one-time survey of birds on installations with habitat for migratory birds would provide the most information to assist compliance with the MOU, the Final Rule, and the NEPA analyses of proposed actions. However, less intensive survey efforts can still be conducted to yield useful information. We describe how various levels of survey effort might be organized and conducted. In addition, continuing surveys, as feasible, would further assist in documenting effects of military readiness and non-readiness activities on species of concern (SOC) (Recommendation 8, Chapter 7).

5. Participation in well-designed, large-scale surveys [(e.g., North American Breeding Bird Survey (BBS; *http://www.pwrc.usgs.gov/bbs/*), Monitoring Avian Productivity and Survivorship (MAPS; *http://www.birdpop.org/maps.htm*)] on land that DoD manages or on lands where the results will be of high interest to DoD, will provide DoD and other NABCI members with information important to bird conservation (Recommendation 9, Chapter 8).

6. Review and implementation of the CBM Plan should involve both higher level management and installation-level natural resources managers (Recommendation 11), be implemented through cooperative partnerships (Recommendation 12), and be followed on U.S territory lands and Army Corps of Engineers projects (Recommendation 10).

Additional recommendations that pertain to implementing the DoD CBM Plan are discussed in Chapter 9.

Chapter 1: Project Summary

This document is the final report under a contract between the Department of Defense (DoD) and the U.S. Geological Survey (USGS). The report describes an approach for bird monitoring, termed the DoD Coordinated Bird Monitoring (CBM) Plan that is intended to ensure that DoD meets its legal requirements for monitoring birds in the most efficient manner possible. The motivation for the report was a determination within DoD that their monitoring programs could be made more efficient and effective through improved coordination, better specification of goals, advice on selection of field and analytic methods, and improved methods for storing and managing the data. Our review showed that the goals and objectives of many DoD monitoring programs are unclear or at least not specified in writing, little rationale is provided for field or analytic methods, and data are usually not contributed to a central repository. In addition, there has heretofore been no agreement on the role of DoD in large-scale, well-designed monitoring programs, nor has there been any specific guidance on how natural resources managers can fulfill DoD's responsibilities under the 2006 Memorandum of Understanding (MOU) with the U.S. Fish and Wildlife Service (USFWS; as required under Executive Order 13186) or the Final Rule regarding migratory birds. The DoD CBM Plan is intended to help DoD address these problems.

Major findings and recommendations are presented in this Chapter. The document then presents a review of current bird monitoring on DoD installations (Chapter 2) and of emerging technologies useful in bird monitoring that DoD has helped support (Chapter 3). These chapters describe the current state of bird monitoring and research on bird monitoring in DoD. The next three chapters are intended for those who conduct or directly supervise bird monitoring programs. They include suggestions for designing short-term monitoring or assessment programs (Chapter 4), selection of field methods (Chapter 5), and storage of monitoring data in long-term repositories (Chapter 6). The final three chapters are intended for policy makers who must make decisions about the general approach DoD will take in bird monitoring. They include a discussion of appropriate monitoring programs for species of concern (Chapter 7), DoD's participation in large-scale bird monitoring programs (Chapter 8), and suggestions for how to implement the CBM Plan throughout DoD (Chapter 9). In the next section below, we describe several recent developments with major implications for how DoD conducts bird monitoring programs.

The U.S. NABCI Report on Bird Monitoring

In February 2007, the Monitoring Subcommittee of the U.S. North American Bird Conservation Initiative (NABCI) released its report "Opportunities for improving avian monitoring" (U.S. NABCI Monitoring Subcommittee, 2007). The report, which was prepared by a distinguished panel of 16 experts in bird monitoring, emphasized the importance of clearly understanding the management questions that monitoring can address before initiating new surveys. The report established four goals and contained four recommendations to achieve these goals (table 1). It also presented a series of action items by which the recommendations and goals could be achieved. DoD, along with the other members of the U.S. NABCI Committee, signed an MOU (U.S. NABCI Committee, 2007) to adopt the goals, recommendations, and action items in the 2007 NABCI Monitoring Subcommittee report that, among other things, states that signatories will "use their best efforts to":

> *Support and promote broad scale bird monitoring programs such as the USGS Breeding Bird Survey (BBS), Monitoring Avian Productivity and Survivorship (MAPS), the Program for Regional and International Shorebird Monitoring (PRISM), and others.*

Table 1. Goals and recommendations in the U.S. NABCI report, "Opportunities for improving avian monitoring."

[U.S. NABCI Monitoring Subcommittee, 2007]

Goal 1. Fully integrate monitoring into bird management and conservation practices and ensure that monitoring is aligned with management and conservation priorities.

Recommendation 1. Establish a policy level expectation that monitoring will be explicitly acknowledged as an integral element of bird management and conservation.

Goal 2. Coordinate monitoring programs among organizations and integrate them across spatial scales to solve conservation or management problems effectively.
Recommendation 2. Take specific steps to increase the appropriate coordination of monitoring programs.

Goal 3. Increase the value of monitoring information by improving statistical design.
Recommendation 3. Every monitoring program should be designed and periodically reviewed in consultation with administrators, managers, and statisticians familiar with bird conservation and survey design.

Goal 4. Maintain bird population monitoring data in modern data management systems. Recognizing legal, institutional, proprietary, and other constraints provide greater availability of raw data, associated metadata, and summary data from bird monitoring programs.
Recommendation 4. Develop a comprehensive plan for integrating and managing bird population monitoring data.

Making DoD monitoring activities consistent with recommendations in the report will ensure that DoD complies with the MOU and follows the best available science. Two other notable recent events in bird monitoring were the signing of an MOU between DoD and the USFWS "to promote the conservation of migratory birds" and the adoption of a Final Rule pertaining to "take of migratory birds by the Armed Forces." The MOU became effective on August 30, 2006; the final rule became effective on March 30, 2007. Both measures include compelling language on the importance of monitoring bird populations. Such monitoring will be critical in assessing the overall impacts of proposed actions on populations of migratory birds, as required per the MBTA (Migratory Bird Treaty Act) /DoD Final Rule and NEPA.

Under the 2006 MOU (table 2), DoD agrees to collaborate with the USFWS and other groups involved in bird monitoring efforts to:
- assess the status and trends of bird populations and habitats,
- use national standards and protocols to the extent appropriate,
- deposit monitoring and inventory data it collects in national repositories, and
- promote participation in national inventory and monitoring programs, such as the BBS.

DoD also agrees that prior to starting any activity that is likely to affect populations of migratory birds it will identify species likely to occur in the area and determine whether any species of concern "could be affected by the activity." Furthermore, DoD agrees to "evaluate the effectiveness of conservation measures to minimize or mitigate take of migratory birds" and to review Integrated Natural Resources Management Plans (INRMPs) to determine whether updates or revisions are needed "to avoid or minimize take of migratory birds."

Table 2. Selected passages from the MOU between DoD and the U.S. Fish and Wildlife Service to promote the conservation of migratory birds.

[Department of Defense, 2006]

D. Responsibilities
1. Each Party shall:
    d. Promote collaborative projects such as:
        (1) Developing or using existing inventory and monitoring programs, at appropriate scales, with national or regional standardized protocols, to assess the status and trends of bird populations and habitats, including migrating, breeding, and wintering birds;
        (2) Designing management studies and research projects using national or regional standardized protocols and programs, such as MAPS, to identify the habitat conditions needed by applicable species of concern, to understand interrelationships of co-existing species, and to evaluate the effects of management activities on habitat and populations of migratory birds;
        (3) Sharing inventory, monitoring, research, and study data for breeding, migrating, and wintering bird populations and habitats in a timely fashion with national data repositories such as Breeding Bird Research and Monitoring Database (BBIRD), National Point Count Database, National Biological Information Infrastructure, and MAPS;
        [(4) Intentionally excluded]
        (5) Participating in or promoting the implementation of existing regional or national inventory and monitoring programs such Breeding Bird Survey (BBS), BBIRD, Christmas Counts, bird atlas projects, or game bird surveys (e.g., mid-winter waterfowl surveys) on DoD lands where practical and feasible.
        (6) Using existing partnerships and exploring opportunities for expanding and creating new partnerships to facilitate combined funding for inventory, monitoring, management studies, and research.
2. The Department of Defense shall:
    d. Consistent with imperatives of safety and security, allow the USFWS and other partners reasonable access to military lands for conducting sampling or survey programs such as MAPS, BBS, BBIRD, International Shorebird Survey, and breeding bird atlases.
    e. Prior to starting any activity that is likely to affect populations of migratory birds:
        (1) Identify the migratory bird species likely to occur in the area of the proposed action and determine if any species of concern could be affected by the activity;
        (2) Assess and document, using NEPA when applicable, the effect of the proposed action on species of concern.
    g. Develop and implement new and/or existing inventory and monitoring programs, at appropriate scales, using national standardized protocols, to evaluate the effectiveness of conservation measures to minimize or mitigate take of migratory birds, with emphasis on those actions that have the potential to significantly impact species of concern.
    i. In accordance with DoD INRMP guidance, promote timely and effective review of INRMPs with respect to migratory bird issues with the USFWS and respective state agencies. During The INRMP review process, evaluate and coordinate with USFWS on any potential revisions to migratory bird conservation measures taken to avoid or minimize take of migratory birds.

Under the Final Rule (table 3), DoD may take migratory birds during military readiness activities, but if DoD concludes that the take may result in a "significant adverse effect on a population" then it must confer with the USFWS "to develop and implement appropriate conservation measures to minimize or mitigate" the effects. If the actions taken include monitoring, then the data collected must be retained for 5 years. If monitoring mutually agreed to by the parties is not implemented, then the Secretary of the Interior can withdraw the take authorization, which would arguably make the military readiness activity in violation of the MBTA when a migratory bird is incidentally taken by the activity.

Table 3. Selected passages from the Final Rule by the USFWS pertaining to "take of migratory birds by the Armed Forces."

[U.S. Fish and Wildlife Service, 2007]

---

§ 21.15 Authorization of take incidental to military readiness activities.
  (a) Take authorization and monitoring
    (1) ...the Armed Forces may take migratory birds incidental to military readiness activities provided that, for those ongoing or proposed activities that the Armed Forces determine may result in a significant adverse effect on a population of a migratory species, the Armed Forces must confer and cooperate with the Service to develop and implement appropriate conservation measures to minimize or mitigate such significant adverse effects.
    (2) When conservation measures implemented under paragraph (a)(1) of this section {§21.15} require monitoring, the Armed Forces must retain records of any monitoring data for five years from the date the Armed Forces commence their action.
  (b) Suspension or withdrawal of take authorization
    (2) The Secretary may ... withdraw ...authorization for take... if the Secretary determines that a proposed military readiness activity is likely to result in a significant adverse effect on the population of a migratory bird species and one or more of the following circumstances exists:
      (ii) The Armed Forces fail to conduct mutually agreed upon monitoring to determine the effects of a military readiness activity on migratory bird species and/or the efficacy of the conservation measures implemented by the Armed Forces.

From the discussion in the NEPA portion of the Required Determinations section of the rule (Federal Register, p. 8949):
  Furthermore, we [USFWS] expect that military readiness activities will rarely, if ever, have the broad impact that would lead to a significant adverse effect on a population of a migratory bird species, even absent the conservation measures that the Armed Forces undertake voluntarily or pursuant to another statue.

The implementation of DoD monitoring programs will provide essential information needed for assessing the impacts of proposed military actions on migratory birds, as required per NEPA. The information obtained would help guide DoD towards more effective and efficient management and conservation of migratory birds, which would reduce the potential for USFWS invoking their prosecutorial discretion in seeking a MBTA violation and protect from possible third party litigation. In support of this effort, DoD has agreed to participate appropriately in regional and national monitoring programs, to assess effects of military readiness activities on bird populations and, if those effects are significant, to undertake various actions including monitoring. When required by the Final Rule, failure to carry out appropriate monitoring could result in suspension of authorization to take migratory birds. In the rest of this report, we make frequent reference to the MOU and Rule and propose numerous measures to ensure that DoD meets its obligations under them.

CBM Plan for the Northeastern United States

The Northeast Coordinated Bird Monitoring (NE CBM; *http://www.nebirdmonitor.org/*) Partnership recently released their "Northeast Bird Monitoring Handbook" (Lambert and others, 2009; *http://www.nebirdmonitor.org/handbook*) featuring "Ten steps to successful bird conservation through improved monitoring" (table 4). Their steps are consistent with the recommendations in this report. For example, steps 1 through 6 are similar to the recommendations in Chapters 4 and 5 of this report, although they contain a number of useful new ideas, such as their emphasis on how the target population relates to "other ecosystem elements, processes, and stressors." Step 7, on data management, contains material similar to the recommendations in Chapter 6. Their steps 8-10 focus on implementation that we cover only briefly (Chapter 9). Overall, the NE CBM Plan provides an excellent companion document to this one. Both can be used at all installations involved in bird monitoring.

Table 4. Ten steps to successful bird conservation through improved monitoring.

[From Lambert and others, 2009]

Step 1: Establish a clear purpose.

Step 2: Determine whether an existing program or protocol meets your needs.

Step 3: Assemble a team of collaborators with complementary interests and skills.

Step 4: Summarize the relationship of target populations to other ecosystem elements, process, and stressors.

Step 5: Develop a sound approach to sampling and data analysis.

Step 6: Design standardized protocols that minimize error and bias.

Step 7: Identify or develop a data management system.

Step 8: Implement the monitoring program.

Step 9: Report results in a format that supports conservation decisions.

Step 10: Use results to make better and more cost-effective management and conservation decisions.

Major Findings of this Study

This section briefly reviews the major findings of this study. More detailed accounts of each part of the study are contained in the remaining Chapters. The review of current monitoring programs (Chapter 2) was conducted by contacting 405 DoD military installations using telephone and email throughout the United States (but not in territories or other countries) and obtaining standardized descriptions of bird monitoring programs that were active during 2002–2004. Descriptions were obtained of 358 monitoring programs from 134 installations. The descriptions were deposited in repositories maintained by Bird Studies Canada, the Laboratory of Ornithology at Cornell University, and the USGS. Many surveys were undertaken as part of the Monitoring Avian Productivity and Survivorship program (MAPS; 29 surveys), the Bird/Animal Aircraft Strike Hazard program (BASH; 25 surveys), the Christmas Bird Count (CBC; 22 surveys), or the Breeding Bird Survey (BBS; 9 surveys). Landbirds were the most common species studied (74 surveys), although waterbirds (22 surveys) and raptors (25) also were often studied. Major conclusions from this project were that documentation of DoD efforts in bird monitoring is poor at present but can readily be improved by requiring that a description of each survey be deposited in the Natural Resources Monitoring Partnership (NRMP; see Recommendation 4 below for description) and by following additional recommendations below. Detailed results from this survey are presented in Chapter 2.

DoD has been a leader in supporting research on bird monitoring and this support has helped not only DoD but many other agencies and organizations carry out effective and efficient monitoring. A brief review of emerging technologies that will lead to additional improvements is provided in Chapter 3.

Guidelines for designing bird monitoring surveys (Chapter 4) included three separate products: a manuscript describing how projects should be planned, guidelines for selecting field methods, and a new USGS database to be used for data management. The manuscript was based on current views of how monitoring should be designed (e.g., Oakley and others, 2003; U.S. NABCI Monitoring Subcommittee, 2007) and stressed explicit identification of goals, objectives, and methods. The guidelines have been published (Bart, 2005) but a slightly modified version stressing DoD applications is presented in Chapter 4.

The guidelines for designing bird monitoring surveys (Chapter 4) and those for selecting survey methods (Chapter 5) were developed to provide DoD natural resources managers and biologists (both employees and contractors) with a single authoritative source that can easily be adapted to their needs and updated as new methods are introduced.

The CBM database (Chapter 6) was created because all existing databases that accept data from throughout the country require that users accept a standardized list of variables; none of them permit the managers of the survey to define their own variables. By contrast, the new "Coordinated Bird Monitoring Database" (CBMD) does permit the managers of each program to define their own variables. The CBMD is maintained by the USGS. The CBMD is meant to be used in combination with the eBird program (for entering fairly simple observations) and the AKN (for storing a reduced set of variables).

An extensive review of existing information on ranges of species of concern (SOC), specifically from the American Bird Conservancy (ABC)/ National Audubon Society (Audubon) Watch List (*http://www.abcbirds.org/abcprograms/science/watchlist/index.html*), was undertaken to identify installations that are used or may be used by these species, especially during the breeding season, or that are major concentration areas for groups of species during the non-breeding seasons (Chapter 7). The review identified 293 installations that probably are used by >70 SOC. We identified 35 installations that probably do not support SOC. This review did not include contacting installation biologists, many of whom undoubtedly know what SOC occur on their installations. The review does show, however, that no comprehensive analysis exists of which installations are important for which SOC. This information is needed for compliance with the MOU and Migratory Bird Rule and other rules and regulations (e.g., NEPA compliance). We provide recommendations for how to carry out brief surveys, partly by using the eBird program, to obtain the needed information.

The following criteria can be used to determine the level of DoD participation in large-scale surveys (Chapter 8): (1) if the lands to be surveyed are under DoD management and are very important to the focal species, then greater participation by DoD will have greater benefits for both the resource and to DoD; (2) if the lands to be surveyed are not under DoD management, but are still very important to the focal species (e.g., on migration or wintering areas), then greater participation by DoD also will have greater benefits for both the resource and DoD.

Recommendations

This section summarizes our recommendations and provides brief explanations and justifications for them. The section is meant to serve as a short, stand-alone summary of the study that provides more detail than is in the Executive Summary.

1. The recent recommendation by the U.S. NABCI Committee (U.S. NABCI Monitoring Subcommittee, 2007) to "establish a policy level expectation that monitoring will be explicitly acknowledged as an integral element of bird management and conservation" offers a useful policy commitment to achieve scientifically based management throughout DoD.

   Although many federal and non-federal programs that influence birds do include monitoring efforts, the NABCI Subcommittee's review indicates that many other programs do not. The recommendations in this report will help ensure that monitoring is appropriately incorporated into all DoD activities. An MOU endorsing the NABCI report was signed by members of the U.S. NABCI Committee, including DoD. Formal DoD policy endorsing the NABCI Subcommittee recommendation and this Plan would be appropriate and beneficial in implementing the goals of this Plan.

2. DoD monitoring programs will maximize scientific validity and success by following the 'Guidelines' presented in Chapter 4.

   A detailed description of what management issue the monitoring program will address, what quantities (e.g., individuals, breeding males, nests) need to be estimated, and what methods will be used — including the sampling plan, data management strategy, and reporting, as well as field methods — is now viewed as an essential component of planning any monitoring program (U.S. NABCI Monitoring Subcommittee, 2007). Following the Guidelines described in this report will ensure that all these topics are adequately addressed.

3. We recommend that DoD natural resources managers consider using the guidelines presented in this report for selecting field methods and contribute to improving them as needed.

   Using of the key presented in Chapter 5, and continually improving it, will ensure that state-of-the-art field methods are selected in DoD bird monitoring programs. This will both ensure that data collection is efficient and will provide a measure of assurance that others cannot successfully challenge the program's results on the basis that the methods used were inappropriate.

4. Preparation of metadata for all DoD monitoring programs and entry into permanent repositories, such as the NRMP database maintained by the USGS Status and Trends Program, will enhance the value and utility of the information collected.

   Metadata is a standardized format for describing datasets including who collected the data and how, what information the dataset contains, and numerous details about the data. The NRMP was developed through collaboration by numerous organizations involved in ecological monitoring and is now recognized as the primary repository for descriptions of monitoring programs and metadata. Entering the description of a program requires only a few minutes by someone familiar with the monitoring program. The information provided makes it possible to quickly and easily retrieve all programs within the database related to a given issue, area, or set of species. DoD participation in the NRMP would be consistent with the MOU and Migratory Bird Rule.

5. Using eBird or the CBMD for data entry and the CBMD and the AKN for permanent data storage will maximize efficiency of processing and guarantee future access to the information collected (see fig. 2 in Chapter 6).

   The eBird program, managed by the Cornell Laboratory of Ornithology, provides a convenient Internet-based method for recording observations made by birders, and steps are being taken to ensure that eBird is available to all DoD personnel. [For more information on eBird, see page 39]. For more complex surveys, we recommend use of the CBMD, which was developed during this project. Virtually any information collected on a "counts survey" (times and places were selected and something was counted) can be stored in the CBMD. The CBMD is a permanent USGS repository so information stored in it will not be lost. The data can be made available by password only (because it would be subject to a Freedom of Information Act (FOIA) request, highly sensitive data should not be stored in the CBMD). If the data owner chooses, core variables will be uploaded from the CBMD to the AKN at Cornell University on a regular basis. The Cornell Laboratory of Ornithology also has offered to make digital or paper copies of all DoD survey datasets and to store them until they are entered into eBird, the CBMD, or the AKN. Accepting this offer from the Cornell Lab would ensure that datasets are not lost. Chapter 6 provides details on how data entry can be accomplished efficiently.

   Having detailed data from DoD installations is important for assessing the population status of migratory birds and will permit assessment of the impacts of proposed military (both readiness and non-readiness) activities on migratory birds, especially at the population level, as required per the MBTA/DoD rule. An accurate assessment will reduce the installation's vulnerability to lawsuits filed under the Administrative Procedures Act (APA).

6. Publishing the results from major monitoring efforts in the peer-reviewed literature will enhance their credibility.

   When awarding contracts or making other arrangements for monitoring projects, DoD may choose to encourage publication of major results. This will help establish their reliability and will help discourage challenges to decisions based on the results.

7. Continuation by DoD of its SERDP and Legacy programs will accomplish a wide variety of avian conservation efforts.

   The Legacy and SERDP programs are widely recognized as making important contributions to bird conservation and bird monitoring in particular. For example, funds from these programs were used by USGS to develop the CBMD and by Cornell University to develop new monitoring techniques based on sophisticated sound recording systems. DoD, as well as the general research and management communities, should consider Legacy and SERDP as important programs that can provide funds to answer DoD-specific questions about bird conservation, and these programs should be considered an essential component of the overall DoD CBM Plan. An increase in Legacy funding to cover unfunded monitoring and other bird-related needs would provide significant benefit to DoD in sustaining its training mission.

8. Appropriate monitoring should be conducted to identify species of concern on installations. A year-round, one-time survey of birds on installations with habitat for migratory birds would provide the most information to assist compliance with the MOU, the Final Rule, and NEPA analyses of proposed actions. However, less intensive survey efforts can still be conducted to yield useful information. In addition, continuing surveys, as feasible, would further assist in documenting effects of military readiness and non-readiness activities on species of concern.

   The Final Rule makes it clear that DoD must determine the impact of military readiness training on migratory birds. This seems to require documentation of what birds are present, in what areas, and at what times of year. Without such information, collected using appropriate methods and archived in a permanent database, DoD cannot show that it has met this requirement, nor can it accurately assess the level of impacts that proposed actions may have on migratory birds. These datasets also will provide the appropriate basis for developing continuing programs to monitor migratory birds that are considered to be at risk from military readiness activities. Installations that have already completed surveys within an appropriate timeframe, and with a standardized sampling methodology, may not need to repeat this. We currently are assessing what is considered "an appropriate timeframe" and the CBM Implementation Plan will provide more guidelines for this topic. Chapter 7 provides suggestions for how to obtain the needed information with different protocols for different levels of available support and existing information on species of concern.

9. Participation in well-designed, large-scale surveys (e.g., BBS, MAPS) on land that DoD manages or on lands where the results will be of high interest to DoD, will provide DoD and other NABCI members with information important to bird conservation (Chapter 8).

   DoD may choose to participate in well-designed, extensive surveys by carrying out the recommended surveys on its own land. However, it might not choose to survey other lands, to participate in poorly designed surveys, or to take the lead in establishing surveys except when it has responsibility for a substantial fraction of the bird populations in question (e.g., some endangered species). For example, DoD might participate in the Intermountain West Aquatic Bird Survey and in the east coast surveys of migrating shorebirds because these are both well-designed, widely endorsed surveys and DoD manages some important wetlands in both of these areas. But DoD should not be expected to take the lead in extending these surveys to other areas. Other agencies (e.g., the USFWS) probably would take the lead in such efforts. It also is becoming increasingly clear that many bird populations are limited by events occurring outside of the breeding season and outside of the United States and that only by studying birds at these times can effective conservation plans be designed. It thus may be cost effective to study species of concern during migration and at wintering areas, as well as outside the U.S., especially in the neotropics. DoD support for such work has been critical in the past. Recommendations on DoD's participation in specific large-scale surveys are discussed in Chapter 8.

10. Implementing the CBM Plan on U.S. territories and other units within DoD may be useful.

    Installations on U.S. territories may benefit by following the DoD CBM Plan. In addition, the U.S. Army Corps of Engineers, which administers approximately 12 million acres of land and water, has done relatively little inventory or monitoring to develop even baseline bird lists (except for some isolated projects that have trained personnel). The U.S. Army Engineer Research and Development Center, Environmental Laboratory, has taken steps (see Guilfoyle and Fischer, 2007) to improve that coordination, but more work in the monitoring arena would be useful.

11. Review of the recommendations in the DoD CBM Plan by upper level management in DoD would be useful with subsequent implementation, as appropriate, on DoD lands.

    At present, most decisions about when, where, and how to carry out bird monitoring activities are made at the installation level. This complicates coordination of bird monitoring activities as required by the MOU and Final Rule. For example, many months were required in this project to conduct the inventory of current bird monitoring and assessment activities whereas it could have been done in a few minutes if descriptions of these programs had been in the NRMP database. Many decisions about when, where, and how to conduct monitoring will remain at the installation level, but decisions about how to design the programs and store the data and decisions about surveying species of concern and participating in large-scale surveys could be made at a higher level (Chapter 9).

12. Following review and revision of these recommendations, as appropriate, the installation-level recommendations could be implemented through a cooperative partnership among DoD and other agencies (e.g., USGS) and non-governmental organizations.

    The recommendations include new procedures for designing short-term surveys, selecting field methods, and storing data in long-term repositories. These recommendations need to be presented, reviewed, and revised as appropriate through a series of consultations at individual installations and at regional meetings for DoD personnel. More detail about how these activities might be carried out is contained in Chapter 9.

Chapter 2: Review of DoD's Existing Bird Monitoring Programs

Many DoD installations across the country have current or recently completed bird monitoring studies. These studies originate from a variety of sources including INRMP documents, BASH programs, requirements under NEPA, state and federal requirements for threatened and endangered species monitoring, and agreements with university research programs. At the start of this project, no comprehensive survey of DoD's bird monitoring programs was available and, as a result, it was difficult to determine how many monitoring programs occur on DoD land, what their objectives are, whether they use appropriate methods, and where the data are stored. We were therefore asked to make a detailed inventory of DoD monitoring programs and to make recommendations for improving the overall value of these efforts. We also were asked to prepare metadata records for the programs, when feasible as recommended by the NBII.

Methods

Chris Eberly, the DoD Partners In Flight (DoD PIF) Program Coordinator, provided a list of installations and contacts from the National Military Fish and Wildlife Association Fish and Wildlife News subscribers list. We modified the list with updated and additional contacts, although there is a considerable amount of turnover and many contacts may no longer be accurate. Attempts to contact all installations were made by phone, email, or both. The following information was requested for each study project: study name, author/originator, brief abstract, purpose of study, years, brief methods, point of contact (name, mailing address, phone, and email). Initially, David Kirk (a contractor for the USGS) gathered similar information by phone and email and entered the results (not including contact information) into the Bird Studies Canada North American Bird Monitoring Projects Database. Later, it was decided to store the information in the NBII Clearinghouse Gateway and still later that the metadata should be stored in the newly created Natural Resources Monitoring Partnership (NRMP) database also maintained by NBII. Metadata records were created using Metavist 2005 version 1.3 obtained from the United States Department of Agriculture (USDA) Forest Service Research & Development. Contact information for each installation will not be included in these publicly accessible records. Instead, the DoD PIF Program Coordinator will be listed as the point of contact and will maintain and distribute more detailed contact information as appropriate.

Results and Discussion

Contact was made with 207 of the 405 installations. Respondents provided information on 358 bird monitoring and/or assessment projects, both long-term and short-term, on 181 installations. We tried to find additional names or phone numbers for installations that did not respond to our request for information by using the Internet but this approach was not productive. We categorized studies into groups and found that most bird monitoring efforts focused on species of concern (SOC; table 5). Detailed data about each program are presented in appendix A.

The information obtained in the metadata records will be useful in many instances including the search for datasets to use in large-scale analyses, finding studies and methods that may be valuable to duplicate in other locations, and increasing interest and participation in future bird monitoring efforts across DoD lands. Considerable time and effort was expended in collecting the necessary information to create metadata records for this project, but it would be very easy for natural resources managers to enter and maintain bird monitoring records for their installation through the NRMP website. Such a database also could be used to answer many of the data calls that at present must be addressed at the installation level. This may provide impetus for managers to keep good records of work planned and completed with the associated datasets, making the data useful beyond the immediate needs of the study project.

Through many of the phone conversations with natural resources personnel, we learned of a widespread interest in having this database available for managers to see what kinds of monitoring other installations were conducting and how they might model their own studies after successful programs. Most data are stored at the point of collection and much is on paper in a file. Many of the biologists we interviewed also commented that they would like a place to store their data (which the NRMP does not do) and that they would like advice on design, selection of field methods, and analysis of data. These issues are addressed in Chapters 4–6.

Table 5. Types of bird monitoring and assessment projects on DoD lands, including projects completed during the last 10 years.

Number of installations	Category
25	Bird/Wildlife Aircraft Strike Hazard (BASH)
29	Monitoring Avian Productivity and Survivorship (MAPS)
9	Breeding Bird Survey (BBS)
22	Audubon Christmas Bird Count (CBC)
1	Breeding Bird Census (BBC)
4	Hawk Watch
29	Nest box monitoring
122	Species of Concern
20	Single species of interest
74	Landbird focus
22	Waterbird focus
25	Raptor focus
30	Other

Chapter 3. Emerging Technologies for Monitoring

As mentioned in Chapter 1, DoD has been a leader in supporting research on bird monitoring, primarily through the DoD Strategic Environmental Research and Development Program (SERDP) and Environmental Security Technology Certification Program (ESTCP), and applied management through the DoD Legacy Resource Management Program . Many of these projects have led to the development of methods useful to DoD as well to the larger conservation community. Here, we highlight a few areas and some of the possibilities for further progress. The few topics discussed are by no means the only areas in which substantial progress is likely to occur soon, but they illustrate the breadth of work now being done to make monitoring more effective. It also should be noted that these sections are intended only to identify some exciting potential methods, not to provide a complete discussion of advantages and disadvantages (which in general are not yet well known) or of all cases in which the methods will or will not be suitable.

Acoustics

Acoustical methods have a prominent role in avian monitoring efforts because many birds can be heard more reliably and at much greater distances than they can be seen. Autonomous data collection using recording devices and automatic data processing and analysis using specially designed software have both revolutionized and expanded the capabilities and application of acoustic technology for monitoring birds. However, several factors impede translation of bird sound detections by humans into reliable estimates of abundance. Human listeners differ significantly in hearing thresholds and psychoacoustic acuity and in their ability to identify sounds, in coping with dense choruses, and in judging distances to bird sounds. Moreover, patterns of bird sound production are not well quantified.

These limitations apply to all acoustic monitoring methodologies, whether ground-based monitoring of diurnal birds or monitoring the flight vocalizations of vast numbers of nocturnal migrants. The best uses of acoustic technologies to address these limitations and to enhance biological and conservation understanding could perhaps best be summarized as the following opportunities:

- to monitor species acoustically that vocalize infrequently,
- to improve accuracy of existing census methods,
- to produce acoustic datasets for training purposes, and
- to monitor flight-calls of migrant birds for predicting migration and stopover use on DoD installations.

Autonomous data collection is critical for any remote or extensive acoustic survey, and digital autonomous recording units (ARUs) can record time-stamped files for months-long periods or longer. These units provide a fundamental and valuable extension to traditional acoustical studies because (1) they can easily detect species that are not efficiently censused by point-count methods because they vocalize infrequently, and (2) ARUs can be deployed in advance at many sites for long durations and programmed to record simultaneously. These devices improve our knowledge of the limiting factors of observers monitoring birds acoustically and of protocols for monitoring birds that may be missed by traditional observation methods. ARUs were used extensively at Fort Hood to monitor endangered Golden-cheeked Warblers (*Dendroica chrysoparia*) and Black-capped Vireos (*Vireo actricapillus*), under SERDP CS-1185, and at DoD facilities nationwide to monitor the species composition and migration phenology of nocturnally migrating birds under Legacy 05-245, 06-245, and 07-245.

Additionally, such devices played a prominent and critical role in the recent search for several rare species (including Ivory-billed Woodpecker, *Campephilus principalis*). Other work by the University of Puerto Rico (Legacy 07-345 and 08-345) is investigating wireless remote automated digital recording systems and community-level identification of species.

Advances during the past decade in processing and analysis methodology include increased computer processor speed, automated detection software, increased data storage capacities, and a comprehensive identification guide. For processing and analyzing audio data containing flight calls, these advances permit recording of the vocalizations of passing migrants over entire nights across seasons, thus yielding data on species composition, migration timing and routing, and the magnitude of migration traffic. Because many North American species of birds give distinctive flight calls during nocturnal migration (likely close to 450–500 species), monitoring flight calls of nocturnally migrating birds is critical for studying the timing and magnitude of migration, as well as for confirming the presence of individual species. A citizen-based project running from 1999 to 2001 used pre-amplified microphones and a Java application that enabled volunteers to automatically detect nocturnal flight calls using the sound card inputs on their personal computers. Nocturnal flight calls were uploaded over the Internet each morning, and logged in a database that hosted graphical tools for reviewing and labeling the sounds. Numbers of migrants detected at night were then compared directly with ground-based censuses from nearby sites to relate the composition of species that passed overhead with those that stopped to use habitats on the ground. These numbers also were compared with WSR-88D (Weather Surveillance Radar, 1988-Doppler; also known as NEXt generation RADar, or NEXRAD) radar imagery, providing information on the species composition of radar-detected migration events. Several recent studies also have used these methods to compare nocturnal flight calls and bird density as quantified by WSR-88D imagery (e.g., Farnsworth and others, 2004). However, numerous challenges still remain to be addressed, including: quantification of birds using acoustic data; relationships between acoustic and radar data; source levels on bird vocalizations; and localization of birds in an acoustic array.

DoD applications. DoD installations require accurate measurements of migratory landbird migration patterns and population sizes. Yet, at most DoD locations, complete year-round migratory bird community inventories have not been completed. ARUs provide solutions and sample data that enhance DoD's capacity to monitor avian resources on and around DoD lands and to analyze and summarize these data. This approach to monitoring provides numerous cost efficiencies for surveys across large, inaccessible or difficult-to-survey areas. The innovative acoustic monitoring network under evaluation in current SERDP and Legacy projects provides tools to monitor migratory activity by species, contribute towards more accurate population estimates for these species, and provide information for more accurate environmental risk assessments (for the MBTA, ESA, and NEPA). In addition to monitoring avian use of DoD lands, acoustic techniques allow monitoring of bird use of airspace at night over and around DoD installations. A network of acoustic monitoring sites documents migratory phenomena that are unobservable by other means, and enable studies that extend beyond the boundaries of DoD installations. These approaches address four challenges confronting DoD:

1. acquiring detailed information to help reduce bird-aircraft strike hazards,
2. supporting the military mission while meeting environmental stewardship and regulatory obligations,
3. engaging broader societal support and solutions for environmental problems, and
4. ensuring mission sustainability by avoiding mission restrictions, delays, and impacts.

Radar

Since the discovery 60 years ago that birds were responsible for some of the puzzling radar echoes dubbed "angels" by the British, radar has proven to be a useful tool for the detection, monitoring, and quantification of the movements of organisms in the atmosphere. Radar can be used to study the movements of birds in the atmosphere during the day and at night at very small spatial scales (1–10 km of a tracking or marine radar), at intermediate spatial scales (10–200 km or the surveillance area of a single weather radar), and at large spatial scales (continent-wide radar network surveillance). Although some new technology exists and is being field tested, most available radars cannot be used to identify birds to species. However, radar can provide information on flight speeds, and this can be used to discriminate different types of birds based on their airspeeds relative to wind speed and direction (e.g., waterfowl and shorebirds, songbirds).

Radar displays show echoes of targets in the radar beam, and a single echo may be produced by a single target or two or more targets in close proximity. Radar has been valuable not only for descriptive studies of daily and seasonal patterns of bird migration and the roosting behavior of birds, but the technique also has been used to answer important questions related to orientation, aerodynamics, and habitat selection of migrants. Within the last two decades, radar has been used increasingly in risk assessment studies related to projects that could potentially impact species that are migratory, endangered, threatened, or of special concern. Most studies have used high-resolution, short-range marine radar and long-range weather surveillance radar.

Marine Radar

Configurations of Small Mobile Radars. Most of the small, mobile radar units used in studies to date have been 5 kW to 60 kW incoherent pulse marine surveillance radars of 3- or 10-cm wave length (X-band or 9410 MHz ±30 MHz and S-band or 3050 MHz ±30 MHz, respectively). Many of the units are used without modification, and the open array antenna that comes with the unit when purchased projects a beam that is narrow (1.0–2.3°) in the horizontal dimension and wider (20–25°) in the vertical dimension. The exact beam dimensions depend on the length of the open array antenna. Because the open array antenna samples a range of altitudes when the radar is operated in a horizontal surveillance mode, the altitude of individual targets cannot be determined. Several approaches have been used to get around this limitation. One involves placing the transmitter/ receiver with the open array antenna on its side and rotating the antenna vertically instead of horizontally. In this configuration, accurate altitudes of targets can be measured, but target track information is limited to targets moving along the axis of the antenna sweep. In some cases, two units are used—one devoted to horizontal surveillance and the other to vertical altitudinal scans. It also is possible to replace the open array antenna with a rotating, parabolic antenna that projects a narrow (2.5–4°) conical beam. When the conical beam is elevated in the horizontal surveillance mode, the altitude of an echo is a trigonometric function of the range of the echo and the angle of antenna tilt. In other cases, a non-rotating parabolic dish can be mounted on top of the transmitter/receiver unit and directed to any elevation angle between horizontal and vertical to measure the altitude of targets.

Each of the above configurations has its advantages and shortcomings. The open array antenna samples a greater air space, but the range of detection is reduced and the altitude of a target in the vertical scan cannot be linked to the track of a target in the horizontal scan. The parabolic antenna samples a smaller volume of atmosphere but has a greater detection range and three-dimensional information on each target can be measured.

Innovations in Small High-Resolution Radars. In the last decade, capture of raw radar data from marine radar and subsequent digital processing enabled automatic tracking of targets detected by the radar while reducing echo return from ground clutter. This innovation has eliminated the time-consuming manual plotting of radar echoes on the radar display, and provides information on target strength, speed of target, direction of flight, and altitude if a parabolic reflector is used. Track histories of individual targets can be stored for additional analysis. However, small targets flying over strong ground clutter are rarely detected because of the clutter suppression.

The latest developments in marine radar represent a radical and innovative departure from current marine radar technology. The new units are monostatic pulse radars that use the Doppler effect to determine target velocities. This is achieved by resolving targets within particular velocity bands by processing received echoes in a bank of narrowband coherently integrating filters. Consequently, the new radar is able to separate targets of interest from clutter because of the targets' different radial velocities. Thus, small targets in clutter can be detected, quantified, and tracked. Although these units have not been evaluated for bird movement studies, this will occur soon as more and more units are produced.

DoD Applications. Small mobile radars are valuable technological tools for the DoD. They can be used to detect dangerous concentrations of birds in the atmosphere on and near military air fields and this information can be used to inform flight operations that serious BASH conditions exist. When this information is gathered over time, it can be used in the development of a BASH plan for the airfield and greatly improve flight safety.

These radars also can be used to assess the best habitats on military installation for migrant birds. Because most birds initiate migratory flights shortly after dark, the radars can provide information on the relative density of migrants departing from different types of habitat. This information combined with on the ground bird census data can be extremely valuable to natural resources managers interested in the conservation of migratory birds.

Weather Surveillance Radar

Doppler Weather Surveillance Radar. The WSR-88D (Weather Surveillance Radar-1988, Doppler)—also referred to as Next Generation Radar (NEXRAD) during the planning and development stages—is the backbone of the national network of weather radars in the United States operated by the National Weather Service (NWS) in the National Oceanic and Atmospheric Administration (NOAA) of the Department of Commerce, DoD (units at military bases), and non-CONUS Department of Transportation sites. There are 155 WSR-88D radars in the nation, including the U.S. Territory of Guam and the Commonwealth of Puerto Rico.

Biological targets in the atmosphere are readily detected by the WSR-88D, and several investigators have detailed its use for studying bird migration, bird roosts, bat colonies, and concentrations of insects aloft. The WSR-88D can be used to quantify the amount of bird migration aloft and has been applied to studies of regional patterns of migration (e.g., Great Lake Region, Northern Coast of the Gulf of Mexico).

The WSR-88D can be used to delimit important migration stopover areas within 60 km of the radar by measuring the density of birds in the beam as they begin a migratory movement (exodus). Within minutes of the onset of nocturnal migration, the distribution and density of echoes in the radar beam can provide information on geographical ground sources of the migrants (migration stopover areas), and satellite imagery can be used to identify the topography and habitat type that characterizes these areas. At a larger spatial scale (that of the surveillance area of a single Doppler weather radar—out to 240 km range), this approach also can be used to delimit locations of post-breeding, nocturnal roost sites of birds, such as Purple Martins (*Progne subis*) and other species. Martins flying toward the roost late in the day generally do so at low altitudes and often fly under radar coverage, however, when they depart the roost near dawn they climb high into the sky and can be easily detected by Doppler.

At a continental scale, the national network of WSR-88D radars can be used to monitor bird migration over the United States on an hourly basis at different altitudes dependent on distance from the radar. The latter achievement is significant because it provides a means of monitoring the season-to-season and year-to-year variation in the patterns of migration at different altitudes for different geographical regions and the nation as a whole.

Because the radar pulse volumes of the WSR-88D are large ($1° \times 1$ km for reflectivity and $1° \times 250$ m for velocity), a given pulse volume often contains birds, bats and insects, and one must use the mean air speeds of targets to discriminate between slow flying insects and foraging bats and faster-flying migrating birds and bats. The lowest tilt of the WSR-88D antenna averages $0.5°$ above the horizontal, and over most of the surveillance the base of the beam is too high to detect low flying birds. The beam width of the WSR-88D is $1°$, and at a distance of 30 km, the base of the beam is 78 m above antenna level (AAL), the center of the beam is 321 m above AAL, and the top of the beam is 564 m AAL. At that distance, the beam width is 486 m wide. This eliminates the possibility of precise altitudinal measurements of targets.

Innovations to the WSR-88D. Beginning in 2008, WSR-88D technology was significantly upgraded. The radar will undergo a series of modifications that will greatly enhance the radar's capability to provide useful information for biologists who choose to study the distribution and abundance of organisms in the aerosphere. The azimuthal resolution of all three moments of data (reflectivity, radial velocity, and spectrum width) will change from $1°$ to $0.5°$, and the range resolution of reflectivity will change from 1 to 0.25 km and match the existing resolution of radial velocity. Doppler data range will increase from 230 to 300 km, and the amount of data collected and transmitted during a volume scan will increase by a factor of about 2.3. In addition to the move toward super-resolution data, the radar will be upgraded to have a dual polarization capability. The latter upgrade provides additional information that can be used to discriminate between return from birds and return from insects.

DoD Applications. The WSR-88D is a valuable technological tool for the DoD. The radar can be used to detect dangerous concentrations of birds in the atmosphere over large geographical areas. This information is extremely valuable for alerting military flight operations of hazardous concentrations of birds along low-level training routes and near military air fields. Information on bird migration gathered with the WSR-88D is being used to develop migration forecast models that can be used to predict when hazardous concentrations of birds aloft will occur. This will allow flight operations at an airfield to schedule training flights when conditions are not favorable for bird migration.

The WSR-88D can be used to determine the locations of important migration stopover areas on or near military bases, and SERDP has funded a project that uses information from the WSR-88D to map important migration stopover areas on and near 50 military installations in the United States. The radar also can be used to determine when migrants are likely to be present on base so that natural resource personnel can census them in different habitats. The density of migration aloft at 10 p.m. local time measured with the WSR-88D correlates significantly with the number of migrant birds captured the next day at a banding station.

Telemetry

Telemetry devices, such as satellite and radio-frequency (RF) tags, play an increasingly important role in understanding bird movements across a spectrum of temporal and spatial scales. No other method for tracking birds can provide the detailed, individual information offered by these transmitters and data loggers. This technology addresses several fundamental questions about bird movements, such as the relationships between movements and energy budgets of individual birds, or understanding the exact location and condition of birds in multiple dimensions (e.g., time, space, biotelemetry). However, numerous challenges remain for implementing satellite and RF tag methods, including reducing tag size and mass, improving coverage for satellite and cellular providers, and increasing battery life. These issues aside, telemetry can be a powerful means of gathering specific and highly detailed information on birds on and away from DoD lands.

The array of different telemetry devices is growing, but the list is best summarized as: satellite-based systems, cellular tracking systems, direction finders, and data loggers. Previous DoD-supported research using some of these technologies includes Legacy projects 95-50100 (American White Pelican, *Pelecanus erythrorhynchos*; Peregrine Falcon, *Falco peregrinus*; Golden Eagle. *Aquila chrysaetos;* Swainson's Hawk, *Buteo swainsoni*; and Ferruginous Hawk, *Buteo regalis*), 95-10049 (Peregrine Falcon), 99-1874 (Broad-winged Hawk, *Buteo platypterus;* White-faced Ibis, *Plegadis chihi*), 00-1874 (Broad-winged Hawk), 03-1875 (White-faced Ibis), 06-292 and 07-292 (Osprey, *Pandion haliaetus*), and 05-243 and 06-243 (Burrowing Owl, *Athene cunicularia*) among others. In addition, SERDP funded research to develop Global Positioning System (GPS) satellite transmitters that were used in many of the Legacy-funded satellite projects.

Satellite-based tracking offers global coverage and rapid data availability, two significant improvements over previous technologies for studying animal behavior. The GPS (receiver) and Argos (transmitter) systems have been operational for over two decades and provide worldwide coverage. The high complexity and relatively rapid power consumption (i.e., a large battery typically is required) of these systems have led to relatively large tag masses (10 g range is the lowest presently available).

An alternative option for individual tracking is to use the global cellular network, also an attractive means to telemeter tag data. Their relatively high data rates enable RF tags to stream many types of data, including live GPS, audio, and video. Biotelemetry sensors even collect information about an animal's pulse, respiration, and wing beat. At least one manufacturer is developing a cellular tag based on commercially available radio components, and academic researchers are attempting to miniaturize such tags. Progress is impeded by the closed cellular system in North America, proprietary standards, and reluctant cellular providers. However, the potential is great: small size and low weight are necessary for deploying on animals too small for currently available satellite-based transmitters. This technology could be invaluable to DoD planners who need detailed information about the location and movements of species of interest. Application would benefit the military mission in numerous cases, particularly for understanding at what altitude and in what locations birds pass through flight training areas.

Traditional radio tracking with directional antennas and hand-held receivers is labor intensive. Automatic direction finding and automatic location finding receiver systems attempt to automate the process. Recent advances in digital signal processing technology have enabled application of sophisticated signal processing algorithms. Automatic tracking would remove the subjectivity of determining signal direction and reduce the amount of intensive field work inherent to radio tracking. Additionally, a new generation of tags, based on 802.15.4 and other low-power physical layer standards, is becoming available. These tags exploit generic capabilities of modern ultra-low power microcontrollers and store data from a wide variety of onboard sensors. A tag can schedule transmission to a fixed base station once it receives that station's interrogating signal, and then rapidly offload its data to the base station when other tags are not transmitting. This system enables data recovery from animals that are difficult or impossible to recapture.

Because of the quality and quantity of information that can be gained and the potential for significant savings of time and effort, development and implementation of these tags warrants additional funding and research by the avian scientific community. A light-level sensor that, when coupled with an accurate clock, yields a system capable of geolocation, may be of particular interest. This approach, which uses the time of local noon and the day length to determine position, yields coarse position estimates, with typical accuracies of ±300 km. Despite its low accuracy, this information can be invaluable in determining the routes and schedules of small long-distance migrants, as there currently are no other means to obtain this information. A very simplified sensor tag with only onboard storage and light sensing could weigh as little as 0.5 g, a mass that would allow this approach to be used on 90 percent of terrestrial bird species and virtually all aquatic birds. This technology has several benefits both to the bird (a low mass transmitter is easier to carry, thus reducing the bias of the data collected) and to the DoD (low cost relative to quantity and quality of information obtained).

DoD applications. Land managers at DoD installations require spatially accurate data on avian habitat use and movement. Wildlife telemetry techniques provide high quality data about bird movements and their energetic condition, numerous cost efficiencies for surveys across large, inaccessible or difficult to survey areas, and, similar to acoustical methods, information for more accurate environmental risk assessments (for the MBTA, NEPA, and ESA) and INRMPs. Benefits to mission sustainability and readiness include:

- identifying movements of migrant and resident birds in time and space in order to reduce bird-aircraft strike hazards,
- meeting environmental stewardship obligations by identifying specific areas and types of habitat use, and
- engaging broader societal support and solutions for environmental problems.

Stable Isotopes

Recent technological advances in the use of stable isotopic signatures make it possible to determine the geographic origins and population connectivity of breeding and wintering populations of migratory birds. Stable isotopes are naturally occurring elements that vary in their atomic weights, and previous studies have shown that animal tissues reflect the isotopic composition of their supporting environment. For example, hydrogen isotope (δD) ratios correlate with the δD of local precipitation patterns. In birds, these δD signatures are incorporated into feathers on the breeding grounds when birds molt in their new plumage prior to migration. Because δD isotopes in bird feathers are metabolically inert after growth, individuals can be sampled during the winter to determine their breeding origin. Combining δD with other isotopes that vary over large geographic distances, such as carbon (δ^{13}C) and nitrogen (δ^{15}N), can provide an accurate method to track migratory birds year-round. Researchers at the Smithsonian Migratory Bird Center [Kirtland's Warbler (*Dendroica kirtlandii*) and other warblers] and USGS (Legacy project 05-241 focusing on shrubland birds) have worked with all of these isotopes previously and have published multiple papers regarding their utility and importance for understanding the ecology of migratory birds.

DoD applications. Department of Defense lands account for nearly 5 percent of Federal lands within the U.S. Managing and protecting populations of species, such as migratory birds, on these lands is challenging because such species spend different parts of the year in geographically disparate localities. Land-use patterns and anthropogenic factors, such as hunting and chemical use at non-breeding grounds (non-DoD lands) and along migratory routes, can have important and profound effects on the year-round condition and survival of birds that breed on DoD lands. Yet, for many migratory birds, we do not know basic information such as the location of their non-breeding grounds or their migratory route. Essential to protecting and understanding fluctuations in the abundance of Neotropical migratory birds breeding on military lands is documenting where these birds spend the non-breeding season and identifying threats to these birds on their non-breeding grounds as well as along the length of their migratory routes. Closing the loop on conservation can help with the protection and sustainment of viable bird populations, thus reducing the potential for listing under the ESA and for military activities to have significant impacts on bird populations. In essence, the more secure bird populations are, the better DoD can avoid potential impacts on mission activities.

Capture-Recapture Modeling

Since 1992, the DoD has played a key role in the development of, and contribution of data to, the largest standardized avian capture-recapture dataset in North America—the MAPS program. Initial goals of MAPS were focused on two demographic parameters, productivity, as indexed from constant-effort capture data, and adult apparent survival rate (survival), as estimated from capture-recapture models. In the early days of MAPS, however, options for capture-recapture modeling were limited, and estimating survival required acceptance of unrealistic assumptions about homogeneity of capture probability and survival among individuals. Few methods existed for estimating population parameters other than survival, and there were no formal methods available for modeling relationships among population parameters or linking population parameters to environmental drivers.

Advances in capture-recapture modeling over the past two decades now make it possible to provide realistic inferences about various population parameters (including, but not limited to, productivity and survival) and links between these population parameters and the environment. These advances have increased the value and scope of the MAPS program for avian monitoring and conservation. Methods for accounting for 'transients' in capture-recapture data, developed in part through funding from DoD's Legacy program, allow estimation of survival that is much closer to actual survival rates of resident birds. Reverse-time capture-recapture models allow estimation of recruitment and population growth rates. Robust-design models allow estimation of population size (which can be age-specific), as well as, temporary emigration and immigration rates.

Capture-recapture modeling continues to be one of the most rapidly evolving fields of statistical ecology. Bayesian hierarchical models that use Markov chain Monte Carlo parameter estimation show particular promise. These new methods make efficient use of sparse data and can be used to address various problems that were difficult or impossible to address using classical techniques. For example, hierarchical models can be used to model relationships between demographic parameters (for example, recruitment and survival), allow for incorporation of spatial or temporal effects, easily handle missing data, and allow inclusion of covariates or random (heterogeneity) effects at various levels. Continued development and application of hierarchical models to avian monitoring data, such as MAPS, should lend new insights into causes of population changes on DoD installations.

DoD Applications. MAPS data and analyses have been used on many installations to develop and refine management strategies for birds. The new methods, however, are providing much greater ability to tailor the findings to specific installations and management issues.

Chapter 4: Guidelines for Designing Short-Term Bird Monitoring Programs

Short-term monitoring, as used in this report, includes both one-time surveys designed to collect information on species composition, timing of use, and relative or absolute density, and monitoring designed to estimate a treatment effect such as the impact of training or habitat alteration on a species of concern. More specifically, short-term monitoring programs may be defined as any survey with a termination date (in contrast to surveys like the BBS that are intended to continue indefinitely). DoD conducts dozens to hundreds of short-term monitoring programs each year so their design must be addressed in any comprehensive approach to bird monitoring.

The guidelines in this Chapter are based on recent literature (Oakley and others, 2003; U.S. NABCI, 2007) that stresses the value of clearly identifying goals, objectives, and methods before field work begins. Some of the material in this chapter is technical. It is intended for specialists carrying out, or responsible for, program design and implementation. Guidelines for preparing each component of the project description (table 6) are described below. The identified elements are intended as suggestions only. Real examples, as indicated later in this report, usually differ somewhat in content and sequence. An example of the steps outlined below is provided at the end of this Chapter.

Table 6. Outline used to describe short-term bird monitoring projects.

A. Description of the Management Issue

B. Survey Objectives

    1. Biological population

    2. Information needed

    3. Quantitative objectives

C. Methods

    1. Brief description

    2. Statistical population

    3. Sampling plan

    4. Training and field methods

    5. Sample size requirements

    6. Analytic methods

    7. Data management

    8. Reports

D. Roles and Responsibilities

Components of a Successful Short-term Bird Monitoring Program

Description of Management Issue

If this section is clear, and especially if only one or a few management decisions are the focus, then the rest of the survey description is relatively easy to complete. If the management issue is not clear, then the rest of the survey description is difficult to conceptualize and complete.

To begin, describe the management issue to be addressed or, preferably, the management decision that the monitoring will help managers make. Examples include what habitat management treatment to apply, minimizing bird-aircraft strikes, specific habitat restoration goals, and whether to grant a species increased or decreased protection. Next, explain the spatial and administrative level at which the project is being organized and why this is the right level. This information is important because it has a substantial impact on survey costs. Conclude with a clear, albeit qualitative, description of the product needed to address the management issue.

Survey Objectives

1. Biological population

   Describe the species to be studied (e.g., migrating shorebirds, breeding waterfowl). Specify which individuals are included (e.g., all birds, only breeders, only residents).

2. Information needed

   Provide as much detail as possible about the information to be obtained in the survey. Species, cohorts, times of year, and habitats of greatest interest should be identified, as should auxiliary information, such as level of disturbance, evidence of breeding, and habitat relationships. Identify the parameters to be estimated in precise, quantitative terms (e.g., density of pairs, trend in abundance, or habitat relationships expressed as regression coefficients).

3. Quantitative objectives

   Specify the accuracy target, expressed as power or as precision [for example, standard errors (SEs), confidence intervals (CIs), and coefficients of variation (CVs)] for each parameter, and discuss how it was chosen. This is frequently a difficult section to write, especially in the early phase of a project, and the target may change as work progresses. Having an accuracy target is important, however, because it provides the basis for calculating sample sizes and, in some projects, for choice of field methods. In some studies, resources are fixed so the objective is simply to maximize precision given the available resources. In such cases, simply acknowledge that this is the situation.

Survey Methods

1. Brief description

   Provide one or two sentences summarizing the survey methods.

2. Statistical population

   Identify the population unit and the statistical population. Population units are usually either individuals (e.g., birds), capture devices exposed for a given amount of time (e.g., a "mist net-hour"), or, most common of all, a location for a specified period (e.g., as in a 3-minute point count or a 30-minute area search). The statistical population is the set of population units about which we choose to make inferences (the population of interest), or from which we sample (the sampled population); these two should be distinguished if they are different. For example, in a point count project, the spatial dimension of the statistical population might be all forested locations on an installation, and the temporal dimension might be mornings without high winds or heavy rain. The population of interest probably would be all possible location-times in the population, but the spatial dimension in the sampled population might be locations along roads and trails.

3. Sampling plan

   Define the sampling plan using standard survey sampling terminology, as in the following example: "Two-stage sampling will be used, with stage one preceded by stratification by habitat. Three strata (probably woodlands, fields, other) will be delineated. Primary units will be locations (i.e., the set of possible survey times at a location), and secondary units will be survey times (at a given location). We anticipate that primary and secondary units will both be selected systematically." Assistance from a statistician familiar with survey sampling may be needed in this phase. (Arrangements are being made for USGS to provide this assistance to DoD personnel.)

4. Training and field methods

   Provide a detailed description of training and field methods. Try to foresee practical problems, how they can be addressed, and how seriously the sampling plan or data collection might be compromised by the problems.

5. Sample size requirements

   Use formulas for sample size estimation and allocation of effort, with multi-stage designs, to estimate the sample size needed to achieve the accuracy target for each parameter. Because minimum sample sizes will differ between parameters (e.g., number of pairs of a species), the final study design will usually be a compromise between costs and meeting most of the accuracy targets.

6. Analytic methods

   Describe the methods to be used identifying issues that may be especially difficult and how they are being addressed in the project design. Extremely detailed accounts are not needed, but demonstrate that careful thought has been given to where the analyses may lead and insuring, insofar as possible, that the data collection will support the most useful analyses.

7. Data management

Describe how the data will be entered, organized, stored and retrieved. State if the data will be contributed to regional, national, or continental repositories (and if not, why not).

8. Reports

Describe when reports will be prepared, what they will contain, to whom they will be provided, and by whom they will be reviewed.

Roles and Responsibilities

Describe who will have responsibility for detailed design, field work, data management, analysis, and communication. Also describe who will support/accomplish the project and how (e.g., contracts, in-house support).

Detailed Example of a Successful Program

Description of Management Issue

Recent surveys on barrier islands along the Florida Gulf Coast have revealed that some species of shorebirds are seldom found where beach nourishment projects have been carried out. This finding is a concern because many shorebirds are thought to be declining. Furthermore, the species using these beaches include a federally-listed species (Piping Plover, *Charadrius melodus*), a state-listed species (Snowy Plover, *C. alexandrinus*), and a subspecies of the Red Knot (*Calidris canutus*) determined to warrant federal listing as Threatened.

Due to these concerns, DoD, specifically the Army Corps of Engineers, consults with the USFWS on potential barrier beach projects in Florida to determine whether the project will affect shorebirds adversely and, if so, what might be done to reduce or mitigate the effects. In these discussions, estimates are needed of the number of shorebirds using the project's impact area. In this project, several contractors will use the protocol described below to estimate shorebird numbers in project areas. They also will provide information on behavior and habitat use of the focal species. This information will be useful in estimating impacts and discussing ways to reduce them. After experience is gained with the protocol it will be reviewed and revised as necessary. If appropriate, the revised protocol will be adopted as a standard approach for assessing shorebird numbers in project areas on Florida's barrier beaches. The goal of the project is thus:

Provide scientifically-sound information on whether proposed beach nourishment projects on barrier islands in Florida will have adverse effects on shorebirds and, if so, how to avoid, minimize, or mitigate the effects.

Objective

Obtain estimates of the mean number of shorebirds present in proposed beach nourishment project areas. Collect data on habitat use and behavior of birds (e.g., roosting, foraging).

Selecting the needed number of surveys requires that we specify a quantitative objective for the estimate of mean numbers present. Because shorebird use differs substantially throughout the year, we suggest the surveys be designed to achieve the accuracy target during each of four seasons: winter, spring migration, breeding, fall migration. The coefficient of variation [CV, i.e., the standard error (SE) of the estimate divided by the estimate], is a reasonable metric (accuracy target) for this purpose.

Although no "standard values" for target CVs are available, we believe in this case that obtaining essentially unbiased estimates with CVs of no more than 0.20 is both desirable and feasible. If the CV for an estimate was 0.20 then the 95-percent confidence interval would be approximately the point estimator ±40 percent. For example, if the estimated mean number of birds present was 20 and the CV was 0.20, then the 95-percent confidence interval for the estimate would be approximately 12 to 28. The methods below are designed to produce essentially unbiased estimates of the mean number of birds present during one season with CVs <0.20. Other parameters will doubtless also be of interest, and many of them can be estimated from the survey data. To keep the sample size analysis from becoming too complex, however, the calculations below are based solely on achieving a CV of the estimated mean for one season <0.20.

Methods

Statistical Population

The statistical population includes the area within which shorebirds are likely to be affected by the proposed project at all times when surveys might be conducted. Potential survey times will be limited by darkness and practical factors. The survey times might thus be defined as weekdays between 9:00 a.m. and 5:00 p.m. throughout the season. This definition assumes the difference between the mean number present during these times and during all times of interest (which, e.g., might include weekends and nights) can be ignored. This assumption should be carefully evaluated. In the example given, excluding weekends might be questioned on the basis that human disturbance levels then might be higher, and the number of birds lower, than on weekdays. In other cases, the reverse might be true due to higher disturbance levels at other publicly accessible sites.

Sampling Plan

We assume that on any survey, the entire project area will be searched. The response variable is the number of birds "present" which we suggest defining as the number present at the start of the survey (i.e., birds that arrive during the survey should be excluded, perhaps by giving them a certain code and excluding them during the analysis). We assume that virtually all birds present will be detected and recorded so there is no need to estimate the detection ratio. Under this assumption, and assuming further that the specified sampling plan is followed, the estimate of mean number present is essentially unbiased using all common sampling plans and analytic methods.

Either systematic sampling or stratified random sampling could be used for selecting survey times. Stratified random sampling is appealing because conditions under which about the same number of birds would be present (e.g., low tide versus high tide) probably could be defined as strata. This would substantially reduce the unexplained variation and would result in smaller SEs compared to a systematic sample of the same size. On the other hand, assuming that covariates (e.g., tide height) are recorded, many of the same advantages could probably be obtained by using a model-based approach for the analysis. In the example given, tide height would be incorporated as a covariable that would help reduce residual variation in the model. The emergence during the past decade of "mixed models" offers an opportunity to gain advantages from both stratified sampling. By using mixed models, surveys can be concentrated in periods of highest use and additional covariables can be incorporated into statistical models. Both stratified sampling and use of mixed models in the analysis, however, require a greater degree of sophistication than employing systematic sampling to select times and treating the results as a simple random sample (the usual approach with systematic samples). The lead investigator, perhaps with consultation from a statistician, should choose the sampling plan and analytic methods, with the requirement that a well-defined sampling plan be used and that the general analytic approach be identified before collecting the data.

Field Methods

As noted above, we assume that a simple area search will suffice to find all birds present. Consequently, no special methods are needed to estimate detection rates. It will be useful to collect habitat and behavior information during the surveys. To do this, the survey area should be partitioned into habitat compartments. We recommend classifying compartments by "landform" and "substrate." Review of the landform types will be needed and can vary if necessary between survey sites (although this will reduce ability to compare results across sites, and such comparisons are recommended).

A preliminary list of landforms is:

1. ocean beach
2. bay beach
3. inlet shorelines
4. spits
5. ebb shoals
6. flood shoals

A preliminary list of substrates is:

1. intertidal
2. mud and sand
3. dry beaches
4. fresh wrack
5. old wrack
6. ephemeral pools

Because some of these compartments will change with tide levels or other factors, maps will need to be updated periodically or separate maps will need to be prepared for each condition that affects locations of the compartments. During surveys, the compartment that each bird is in will be recorded along with its behavior. Preliminary behavior codes are roosting and non-roosting. Immediately after the survey, the surveyor will record disturbances during a specified period (e.g., 1 hour). A list of events that constitute a "disturbance" will be continuously developed along with a list of birds' responses to disturbances. The number of disturbances and responses, by type, will be recorded during the observation period.

As noted above, two general approaches for the analysis are available: "design-based" and "model-based" methods. The design-based methods require few assumptions and are straightforward applications of survey sampling theory. For example, if stratified sampling is used to select survey times then the estimate of the mean number present is:

$$\bar{y} = \sum_{h=1}^{L} w_h \bar{y}_h \ , \tag{1}$$

where $\bar{y}_h$ is the simple mean of the surveys in stratum h, w_h is the proportion of all times (not surveys) in stratum h, and L is the number of strata. The standard error of the estimate is:

$$SE(\bar{y}) = \left(\sum_{h=1}^{L} w_h^2 s^2 (y_{hi}) / n_h \right)^{0.5}, \tag{2}$$

where y_{hi} is the number of birds recorded on the ith survey in stratum h, $s^2(y_{hi})$ is the sample variance of the y_{hi}, and n_h is the number of surveys in the hth stratum. Degrees of freedom (df) may calculated using Satterthwaite's method (Cochran, 1977). The 95-percent confidence interval is: $\bar{y} \pm t_{df,.05} se(\bar{y})$.

Numerous model-based methods could be devised. The most obvious is to construct a multiple (mixed) linear regression model that predicts number present as a function of such factors as date, time of day, tide height, and perhaps other factors (e.g., disturbance, weather). The model would then be used to predict number present under average conditions or under a representative sample of conditions (and the outputs would be averaged).

Sample Size Requirements

Sample size requirements will be much easier to estimate after a few years of data have been collected. Estimates made now should be viewed as preliminary. These cautions notwithstanding, an effort was made to predict needed sample size using data collected in the International Shorebird Survey (ISS) in Florida. We assumed that simple random sampling was used. For this method,

$$CV(\bar{y}) = \frac{SD(y_i)}{\bar{y}\sqrt{n}} \tag{3}$$

Setting the CV equal to 0.2 and solving for n yields

$$n = \frac{1}{0.04} \left(\frac{SD(y_i)}{\bar{y}} \right)^2 \tag{4}$$

We used the ISS data to estimate the quantity $SD(y_i)/\bar{y}$ and then calculated the needed number of surveys using expression (4). The results were expressed as a function of mean number present. We used all species, years, and sites surveyed in Florida, and we analyzed four periods separately (November–March, April–May, June–July, August–October). Estimates of $SD(y_i)/\bar{y}$ were only calculated when at least six surveys had been conducted and the mean number present was >0.5 birds.

Results were analyzed by season and species. A typical result is shown in figure 1. It can be seen that the needed number of surveys increases rapidly as the mean number present drops below about three.

Figure 1 should be viewed with caution because the surveys probably were not made according to a well-defined sampling plan and it is difficult to assess how this affected $SD(y_i)/\overline{y}$. If there was little affect on $SD(y_i)/\overline{y}$, then figure 1 probably over-estimates sample size requirements both because stratified sampling probably will be more efficient than simple random sampling (as explained above) and/or because a model-based approach for estimating $\overline{y}$ will be more efficient than a design-based approach. Given these facts, and based on examining other graphs like figure 1, we suggest that 20 surveys probably will be sufficient to achieve the accuracy target in most cases and that 10 surveys per period might be sufficient. If very few birds are present, then more surveys (either more locations or more surveys/location) may be needed to achieve the accuracy target although it also might be argued that the target should be relaxed if hardly any birds are present (i.e., there is less "resource" at risk).

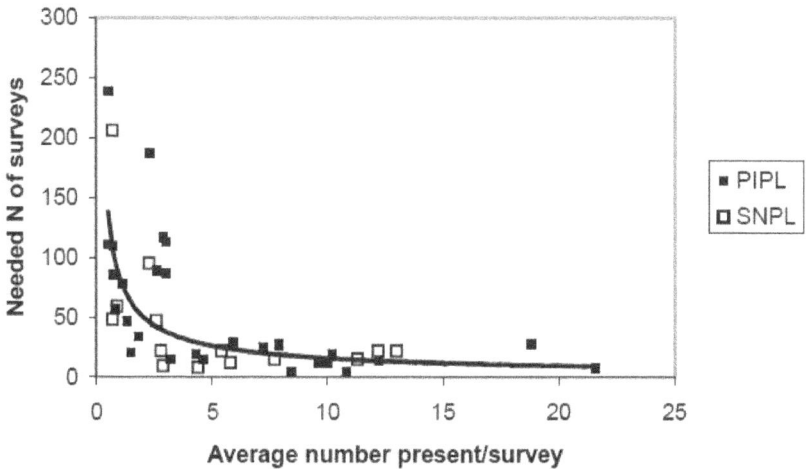

Figure 1. Estimates of the number of surveys needed for CV=0.2 based on surveys of piping plovers (PIPL, *Charadrius melodus*) and snowy plovers (SNPL, *C. alexandrinus*) in Florida during October–March.

Data Management

It is recommended that copies of the data be deposited in a permanent repository, such as the CBMD. This database offers password protection, if desired, query and analytic tools, and optional periodic uploading of core variables to the AKN.

Reports

We recommend brief, quarterly reports for project sponsors that state how many surveys were conducted and that the data have been deposited in a permanent repository, and that discuss preliminary findings as appropriate.

Roles and Responsibilities

The contractor will bear all responsibilities for the bird surveys. Oversight will be provided by DoD.

Concluding Comments

We believe that many project managers would have difficulty completing an example in the detail above. For this reason, a short-term, follow-up Legacy project has been initiated to investigate how best to implement the DoD CBM Plan. It involves providing free technical assistance to help project managers design their monitoring studies following the guidance above. Anyone interested in these services may contact the senior author at *jon_bart@usgs.gov* or (208) 426-5216. Following completion of the Legacy project, a decision will be made about whether to (1) continue the service on a DoD-wide basis (not using funds from Legacy),(2) maintain the service but have individual bases support it as needed, or (3) terminate the assistance program.

Chapter 5: Selecting a Survey Method

This Chapter describes a general approach for selecting field methods. Often, military natural resources managers contract out avian monitoring work and rely solely on the contractor to determine the appropriate type and level of sampling effort. It would be prudent to use this CBM plan as a tool to guide development of management objectives and sampling method and the terms of the contract specifying work to be accomplished.

We believe three objectives (i.e., reasons for conducting surveys) are especially common in DoD surveys: (1) preparing a bird checklist, (2) estimating the number of birds at colonies, and (3) estimating density or abundance of non-colonial birds. The user considers a series of questions until a reasonable method has been identified. The type of data needed depends entirely on the management issues being addressed. Identification of what parameter to estimate is covered in Chapter 4. Here, we assume this decision has already been made and that the answer is one of the three objectives above.

Readers will note that we do not include "estimate change in density (or abundance)" as a goal. Consistent with much of the current literature on bird monitoring (Northeast Coordinated Bird Monitoring Partnership, 2007), detection rates should be estimated as part of bird surveys rather than using index methods. Thus, estimating change in density (e.g., before and after a treatment) involves two efforts to estimate density and does not need to be identified as a separate parameter.

We have prepared these guidelines for wildlife biologists, particularly those in the Department of Defense, who are not specialists in bird monitoring methods. When a large or long-term project is being planned, we recommend consulting a specialist in bird monitoring. Many projects are small and short-term, however, and budget restrictions may hinder finding expert assistance. We hope the guidance in this chapter will be useful in these cases.

The questions below resemble a dichotomous key but there are a few differences in the numbering system. "Checklist" means a list of birds with indications of general abundance at each time of year. Checklists are often developed just with input from experienced birders rather than formal surveys.

1. Select Objective

    Prepare a bird checklist..2
    Estimate number of birds at a colony 3
    Estimate density or abundance other than at a colony.....4

2. Prepare a bird checklist

    Based solely on birders' input 2.1
    Surveys...2.2
    Birders input and surveys ....2.1 & 2.2

2.1 Prepare checklist based on birders' input

    Good birders, knowledgeable about the area can be located through the American Birding Association (*http://www.americanbirding.org/*) or a local bird club or Audubon chapter.

2.2 Prepare checklist based on surveys

Area search surveys should be conducted in all parts of the area to which the checklist applies and at all times of year. Records should be kept of each area surveyed and results should be summarized by calculating the number of individuals recorded per unit time (e.g., 1 day = 8 hours) in appropriate habitat. Such data provide a good basis for defining the abundance categories and assigning birds to them in each season. These records also provide a good basis for describing habitat associations.

3. Estimate number of birds at a colony

Counts of nests are feasible 3.1
Counts of nest are not feasible..3.2

3.1 Colony surveys where counting nests is feasible

Nesting is synchronous or is asynchronous but re-nesting is rare
- In this case making the count at a single time should give an essentially unbiased estimate with suitable precision, assuming resources are available to count the entire colony or a large enough sample from it. If a complete count is possible, then we recommend this approach. If detecting nests is relatively easy but the colony is too large to count completely, then a line transect approach with distance-sampling may be the method of choice. This method assumes that all nests on the transect line are detected; if the assumption is not valid, then it may be preferable to subdivide the colony into plots and count nests in randomly selected plots. These plots should then be searched thoroughly. If not all nests are detected in the random plots, then a method to estimate the detection rate of nests (e.g., double sampling) should be employed.

Nesting is asynchronous but re-nesting is common
- Accurate estimates of the number of nesting birds in the colony can only be made through repeated surveys and by marking some birds to estimate how many nests they initiate.

3.2 Colony surveys where counting nests is not feasible

Birds can best be counted when they leave the colony.
- Use "flightline counts" to obtain an index to colony size.

Birds can best be counted while they are at the colony.
- Count birds when they are at the colony.

4. Estimate density or abundance of non-colonial birds.

One of the methods in table 7 is suitable ....Use that method
None of the methods in table 7 is suitable ....See notes below

When no method in table 7 is suitable, then a form of double-sampling may be useful. In this approach, a rapid method is used to survey a large sample of locations and intensive methods are used on a subsample of the locations to obtain actual numbers present. The ratio of the estimate to the true number present, based on the subsample of locations, is then used as the detection rate on the rapid surveys. Advice from a specialist will normally be needed to design a double-sampling survey.

Table 7. Survey methods and required assumptions.

---

1. Area search

Plots are searched at least once. Surveyors are not constrained to survey pre-determined points or transect, but must search the entire plot. This method assumes all birds are detected or that the same fraction of birds present is detected in groups of plots being compared.

2. Fixed radius point counts

Points are randomly selected and surveyors spend a pre-determined amount of time at each point. Birds judged to be within a fixed distance (e.g., 50 m, 100 m) are recorded. The main assumptions are that (1) the points can be accessed, (2) birds are correctly classified as inside or outside the threshold distance, and (3) all birds within the threshold distance are recorded.

3. Distance

Randomly selected points or lines are selected and surveyed following a protocol that specifies time per point or speed in moving along the transect. For distance-based points counts (point-transects), record the difference from the observer to the detected bird(s). If using distance-based transects, perpendicular distances from the transect to detected birds are recorded, or are calculated using (1) the distance from the observer to the birds and (2) the angle between the compass bearing of the transect and the compass bearing to the bird(s). The main assumptions are that (1) points or transects can be accessed, (2) at least 75 detections will be made of each species, (3) all birds at the survey points or on the transects are detected (or that an unbiased estimate of the proportion of them detected can be obtained), (4) birds do not move prior to detection in response to the surveyors, and (5) distances and angles are accurately estimated. The last assumption means that birds or their locations must be seen by the surveyors.

4. Double observer

Surveyors work in pairs either independently or with detections made by one surveyor being revealed to the other surveyor. The main assumptions are that (1) points can be accessed, (2) any reduction in sample size due to surveyors working in pairs is acceptable, and (3) birds have the same detection probabilities (within surveyors). The last assumption is violated if some birds are quite obvious (e.g., due to persistent vocalizing or proximity to the surveyors) whereas others are hard to detect.

5. Removal methods

The survey period is divided into sub-periods and surveyors record which sub-period each bird is first recorded in. The main assumptions are that (1) points can be accessed and (2) detection events are independent in different sub-periods. The last assumption is often difficult to meet. It means, for example, that birds detected by ear do not sing in bouts.

6. Methods based on capture-recapture theory

The method is similar to the removal methods except that surveyors record every sub-period within which each bird is detected. The main assumptions are that (1) points can be accessed, (2) recording every bird detected in every sub-period is feasible, and (3) detection events for birds assigned to the same "cohort" are independent in different sub-periods. Approximately the same independence assumption is required (e.g., if many birds are detected by their vocalizations then birds must not sing in bouts).

Chapter 6: Data Management

As emphasized recently by the U.S. NABCI Committee and most specialists in avian monitoring, a critical need exists to ensure that monitoring datasets are collected and preserved in long-term repositories to prevent data loss. At a meeting to discuss the DoD CBM plan in Denver in early March 2008, a general approach was defined for insuring that DoD monitoring data are preserved and made available when appropriate (table 8). Table 8 presents a capsule summary of the process but more detail is provided in the section titled "Coordinated Bird Monitoring Database."

eBird

What is eBird?

A real-time, online checklist program, eBird has revolutionized the way that the birding community reports and accesses information about birds. Launched in 2002 by the Cornell Laboratory of Ornithology and National Audubon Society, eBird provides rich data sources for basic information on bird abundance and distribution at various spatial and temporal scales. eBird's goal is to maximize the utility and accessibility of the vast numbers of bird observations made each year by recreational and professional bird watchers. It is amassing one of the largest and fastest growing biodiversity data resources in existence. For example, in 2006, participants reported more than 4.3 million bird observations across North America. The observations of each participant are combined with those of others in an international network of eBird users. eBird then shares these observations with a global community of educators, land managers, ornithologists, and conservation biologists. In time, these data will become the foundation for a better understanding of bird distribution across the western hemisphere and beyond.

How Does it Work?

eBird documents the presence or absence of species, as well as bird abundance through checklist data. A simple and intuitive web-interface engages tens of thousands of participants to submit their observations or view results through interactive queries into the eBird database. eBird encourages users to participate by providing Internet tools that maintain their personal bird records and enable them to visualize data with interactive maps, graphs, and bar charts. All these features are available in English, Spanish, and French.

A birder simply enters when, where, and how they went birding, then fills out a checklist of all the birds seen and heard during the outing. eBird provides various options for data gathering including point counts, transects, and area searches and bulk upload of large datasets. Automated data quality filters developed by regional bird experts review all submissions before they enter the database. Local experts review unusual records that are flagged by the filters. Installation bird checklists could be generated by doing year long surveys using point or area counts and entering data into eBird and generating a species frequency list.

Table 8. Recommendations to the Department of Defense (DoD) for management of historic records, inventory, and new monitoring projects.

[Data curation levels indicate a hierarchy of security, which increases as the level number increases]

---

1. **Data Curation**
   a. Level 1
      i. Identify and gather all existing DoD datasets (see following section for whom to contact regarding collection of data).
      ii. Archive the datasets (i.e., in their original format) at Cornell Lab of Ornithology.
      iii. Complete metadata descriptions of the Level 1 datasets
      iv. Enter metadata into NRMP (for many projects this is complete).
   b. Level 2
      i. Organize all existing DoD datasets into a single standardized data structure. Most of the existing datasets are stored in disparate data structures. Using the AKN Bird Monitoring Data Exchange (BMDE) all existing datasets will be brought into a single data framework.
      ii. A complete metadata description will be made available to the AKN.
      iii. Access to data will be restricted. Backups of the warehouse are made using persistent data archive techniques. AKN data managers will use all data backup options consistent with the goal of no data loss. Backups will undergo periodic data integrity testing. For each data set, a "data owner" will be established within DoD. No applications will access DoD data without specific consent from the data owner.
   c. Level 3
      i. With consent from DoD, Level 2 data will be made available for specific analyses.
      ii. The primary data warehouse serves as the Level 2 data archive, and no applications connect directly to the warehouse. Instead, with prior DoD approval, DoD data will be transferred to separate data views created specifically to optimize the performance of an application that connects to it.

2. **DoD Coordinated Bird Monitoring Database**
   a. Ongoing and new monitoring projects will use the DoD CBM data gathering applications and database.
   b. The DoD CBM database will provide a complete archive consistent with the goal of no data loss.
   c. Complete all metadata descriptions of the Level 1 datasets.
   d. Metadata will be entered into NRMP (for many projects this is complete).
   e. All DoD CBM data sets will be translated to BMDE format and added to the AKN primary data warehouse.

3. **DoD eBird**
   a. Bird inventory data will be collected through DoD eBird when appropriate
   b. The DoD eBird will be archived with the goal of no data loss.
   c. Complete all metadata descriptions of the Level 1 datasets.
   d. Metadata will be entered into NRMP (for many projects this is complete)
   e. All DoD eBird will be translated to BMDE format and added to the AKN primary data warehouse.

4. **DoD MAPS**
   a. Avian demographic data will be collected through DoD MAPS when appropriate
   b. The DoD MAPS will be archived with the goal of no data loss.
   c. Complete all metadata descriptions of the Level 1 datasets (recommendation is for Federal Geospatial Data Committee (FGDC) Biologic Data Profiler).
   d. Metadata will be entered into NRMP (for many projects this is complete)
   e. All DoD CBM MAPS will be translated to BMDE format and added to the AKN primary data warehouse.

Data Integration

eBird collects observations from birders through portals managed and maintained by local partner conservation organizations. In this way, eBird targets specific audiences with the highest level of local expertise, promotion, and project ownership. Portals may have a regional focus (aVerAves, eBird Puerto Rico) or they may have more specific goals and/or specific methodologies (Louisiana Winter Bird Atlas, Bird Conservation Network eBird). A DoD eBird portal is under development. Each eBird portal is fully integrated within the eBird database and application infrastructure so that data can be analyzed across political and geographic boundaries. For example, observers entering observations of Cape May Warbler (*Dendroica tigrina*) from Puerto Rico can view those data separately, or with the entire Cape May Warbler dataset gathered by eBird across the western hemisphere.

Data Accessibility

eBird data are stored in a secure facility and archived daily, and are accessible to anyone through the eBird web site and other applications developed by the global biodiversity information community. For example, eBird data are part of the AKN, which integrates observational data on bird populations across the western hemisphere. In turn, the AKN provides eBird data to international biodiversity data systems, such as the Global Biodiversity Information Facility (GBIF). In this way, any contribution made to eBird increases our understanding of the distribution and abundance of birds.

The Coordinated Bird Monitoring Database (CBMD)

The CBMD is a general "counts database" intended to hold data from a wide variety of surveys in which places and times were selected and then something was counted (fig. 2). The basic format involves a "surveys" table (description of the times and places), a "records" table (description of the things counted) and a "pedigree" table (optional description of the sampling plan). Core variables are defined, and their format is standardized (although the variables are optional). Each dataset has a "data owner." This person defines as many variables additional to the core variables as they choose and decides whether restrictions will be placed on distribution. The CBMD uses the same five levels of access as used by Cornell Laboratory of Ornithology for eBird.

The CBMD is maintained by the USGS Forest and Rangeland Ecosystem Science Center (FRESC) in Boise, Idaho, and made available to all interested parties free of charge. When someone is interested in using the database, they contact the CBMD whose staff then works with them to define their program-specific variables and their sampling plan (if any). If requested, CBMD staff also can produce a Microsoft© Excel spreadsheet for data entry. It usually resembles the field survey forms and contains all variables entered on the form. The spreadsheet has all error-checking rules built into it and programs to reformat the data into the tables ready for upload into the CBMD. The user enters data and then clicks a "Submit" button, which activates the error checking routine. If no errors are found, the data are re-arranged into a format suitable for inclusion in the "surveys," "records," and "pedigree" tables mentioned above and appended to these tables. Periodically, for example at the end of each field season, the spreadsheet is emailed to the CBMD staff who uploads the data into the CBMD.

People can access the data through the Internet. They sign on; choose their program, and enter a password if needed. The variables in the program are then displayed and the user can define a query by selecting any values on any subset of the variables. The user also can query for either a bulk download of all records meeting their query or can query for estimated densities and population sizes for any "level" in the sampling plan. For example, if a user signed on to the Intermountain West Aquatic Bird

Survey, they could query for estimated means and totals (for any subset of records) for each State, each BCR, each "Bird Conservation Subregion" (polygons formed by intersecting a BCR and States/Provinces layers), or each site. They also could query for estimates at the next level below the Site but this would be most useful if they had one or two sites in mind and therefore knew what were the next levels down. This ability to aggregate results in a statistically rigorous fashion, even though many different sampling plans were followed at different sites is, to the best of our knowledge, unique among databases.

The CBMD is a node of the AKN and uploads core variables to it periodically (if the data owner requests this free service). CBMD staff prepare metadata (using both the full FGDC standards and the reduced NRMP set of variables) and submit them to the appropriate permanent repositories maintained by the government and by the Cornell Laboratory of Ornithology. All services related to the CBMD are free. For more information, visit the CBMD web site, *http://cbmdms.dev4.fsr.com/Default.aspx*.

Data from designed DoD monitoring and assessment programs will be entered in the CBMD. Variables suitable for eBird and for the AKN will then be uploaded to these programs. Similar uploads can be made to other repositories if DoD chooses. Birders collecting data on DoD land are encouraged to submit their observations directly to eBird (see *http://ebird.org/content/dod*). Existing datasets should be archived to ensure they are not lost. The Cornell Laboratory of Ornithology has offered to perform this service.

A final comment is that all of these services require access to the eBird, AKN, and CBMD web sites. In addition, DoD pays for access to Birds of North America Online, which resides on the same system as eBird and AKN, for every installation with an INRMP. It is our understanding that some installations are blocked from being able to access these capabilities. Relaxing such restrictions would be helpful to the purposes to which this report is directed.

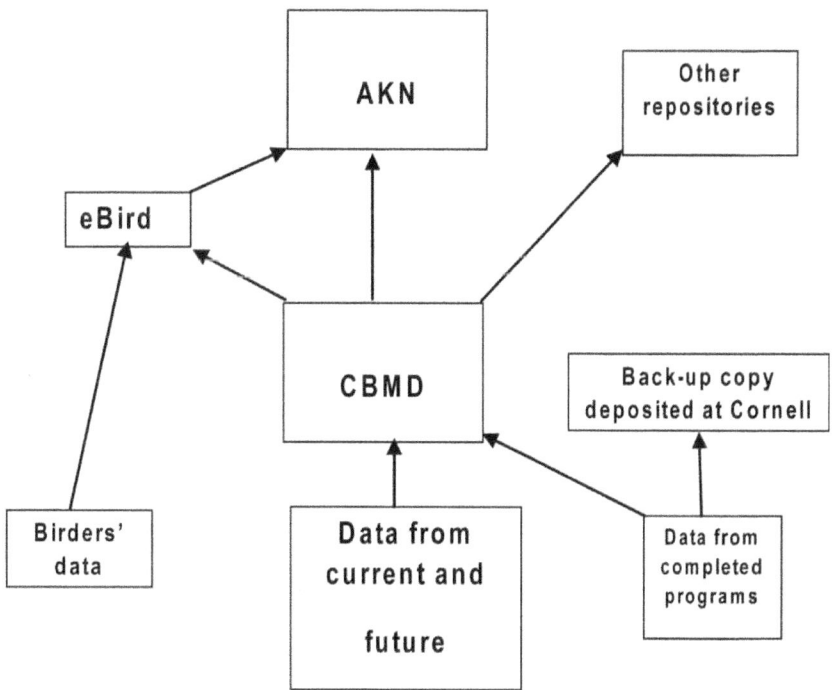

Figure 2. Data management in the DoD CBM program.

Chapter 7: Recommendations for Surveying Species of Concern

The third deliverable to be produced in this report was "a plan for monitoring bird Species of Concern on DoD land." We prepared this plan by identifying DoD installations that have—or may have—Species of Concern in substantial numbers for at least a part of the year. We then developed guidelines for deciding which of these locations should be surveyed and how these surveys might best be conducted.

Methods

For purposes of generating an initial list of focal species, we identified SOC using the ABC and Audubon Watch List (American Bird Conservancy and National Audubon Society, 2007) except that exceedingly rare species were excluded. We included DoD installations in the United States and its' territories and protectorates (e.g., Northern Mariana Islands).

The WatchList is representative of the SOC database on the DoD Partners in Flight web site (*http://www.dodpif.org/*), which was undergoing revisions due to changing assessments in several of the initiative or FWS lists. Regardless of the method used, this SOC identified in table 9 is only a subset of what occurs on DoD installations. In some cases, baseline surveys have not yet been completed, or baseline surveys that have been completed are filed away and not accessible for analysis or review. DoD can greatly advance its monitoring of bird species of concern by completing baseline surveys for all installations, and more importantly, by entering all survey, inventory, and monitoring data into an electronic repository so the data are accessible for such analyses. An initial estimate of the species occurring on each installation in the 50 U.S. States was made by intersecting maps of these installations with maps of each species' range as depicted by Ridgely and others (2007). We then revised these lists using the SOC database from the DoD Partners in Flight website, factsheets describing Important Bird Areas, bird checklists provided by the USGS (Igl, 1996), and important shorebird sites identified by the Western Hemisphere Shorebird Reserve Network (*http://www.whsrn.org/*).

SOC on installations in Hawaii were identified using a combination of bird checklists from the USGS (Igl, 1996), digitized range maps of forest, sea and Nene habitat maps obtained from the State of Hawaii (*http://hawaii.gov/*) and the Rim of the Pacific Programmatic Environmental Assessment of 2002 (*http://www.dtic.mil*). Species of Concern on installations in Guam, Tinian, and Farallon de Medinilla were identified using the Final Environmental Impact Statement for Military Training in the Marianas Volumes One and Two (*http://www.dtic.mil*) and confirmed on guampedia (*http://www.guampedia.com*). Data for one Puerto Rico base, U.S. Naval Security Group Activity Sabana Seca, were obtained from an environmental assessment (*http://www.dtic.mil*).

The draft species lists were sent to editors in the eBird Program for review and revision. We also asked them to identify concentration sites for groups of species during the non-breeding periods. The result was a comprehensive list of installations with species and groups of species that may occur on each.

Table 9. Number of DoD properties with significant concentrations of migratory birds for at least a part of the year and numbers of properties known to contain at least one Species of Concern (SOC).

DoD Entity	Number of Properties	Waterfowl	Shorebirds	Raptors	Herons, etc.	Landbirds	SOC
Air Force	71	22	30	18	8	9	49
Army	39	11	12	5	4	10	30
Army Corps[2]	48	29	19	21	20	26	39
ARNG	30	6	8	6	5	9	25
Joint Reserve Base	1	1	1	1	1	1	1
Marine Corps	17	7	5	0	0	0	13
Navy	87	51	48	1	19	14	53
Total[1]	293	127	123	52	57	69	210

[1]These data are not comprehensive since installation managers were not contacted directly. Many more SOC occur on installations than indicated in this table—this only serves as a cursory guide and suggests much more comprehensive work is necessary to complete this particular table.

[2]Army Corps of Engineers properties are shown to illustrate their potential contribution to bird monitoring efforts within DoD.

Results

We identified 245 military installations and 48 Army Corps civil works sites with suspected or known SOC or significant concentrations of birds of any species (table 9). We included concentrations at all times of year because the new MOU and Migratory Bird rule do not restrict consideration to any portion of the year. We determined that SOC probably do not occur on 35 installations. More than 70 species (or in a few cases other taxa) of special concern are known to occur on the 293 facilities we surveyed.

Discussion

We were unable to obtain completely reliable lists of the SOC and concentrations of migratory birds on each installation. Despite these uncertainties, however, the analysis showed that a great many DoD installations, probably >300, are used by SOC or significant concentrations of migratory birds. It appears that these installations are used by >70 SOC.

As discussed in Chapter 1 of this report, the MOU for migratory birds between DoD and the USFWS includes the following provision (see table 2).

> *Prior to starting any activity that is likely to affect populations of migratory birds [the Department of Defense shall]: (1) Identify the migratory bird species likely to occur in the area of the proposed action and determine if any species of concern could be affected by the activity; and (2) Assess and document, using NEPA when applicable, the effect of the proposed action on species of concern.*

Thus DoD is required to determine effects of its activities on SOC.

This requirement implies that DoD must identify installations (a) that may be used by SOC and (b) on which activities may occur that are likely to affect these species. The only credible way to determine if activities do affect particular species is to have information about their status prior to the activity deemed likely to affect them. This, in turn, requires surveys to identify what species are present and to gather at least basic information on their abundance prior to carrying out the activities that may affect them. Two sorts of surveys (whose results could be combined) probably would be most efficient: initial surveys to determine what SOC, if any, are present on each installation and then follow-up surveys to determine the status of SOC.

It is our recommendation that initial surveys should be approached based on the ability of an installation to obtain funding and/or personnel to complete surveys. A description of survey efforts are described below in hierarchical order based on funding and other capabilities of individual installations.

1. **Year-Round Monthly Surveys**. The preferred method would be to conduct surveys throughout the year. This approach can be very rapid if conducted by an experienced bird surveyor. Although we have not conducted statistical power analyses, based on extensive experience with this sort of survey, we believe that about 12 surveys should suffice with increased intensity during periods when the birds are present or their behaviors are changing rapidly. One reasonable design under this first option would be 4 surveys during the breeding season; 3 surveys during the fall migration; 2 winter surveys (early and late-winter), and 3 surveys during the spring migration. Small installations should be covered completely because doing so will be relatively easy and inexpensive, but on larger installations stratification by habitat and perhaps accessibility will be needed. A few person-days per survey should suffice for small to medium-sized installations, although more effort may be needed on larger installations especially where SOC are known or suspected to be present. If surveys have already been conducted, then additional ones may not be needed. We recommend a simple area-search method, in which observers record estimated numbers of each species encountered. This method is easier for many surveyors than point counts and easier to fit into habitat-based sampling plans. Point counts, however, also could be used. On small to medium-sized installations design of the survey should be simple but on larger ones some detailed planning may be needed to ensure efficiency and that extrapolation to the entire installation is feasible.

2. **Four-season Surveys**. The next preferred level of effort would include a 4-season survey, with surveyors conducting point counts or area searches, as described above, once each during spring, summer, fall, and winter seasons. Point count surveys that are distributed throughout small to medium-sized installations, and stratified by habitat on larger installations, also are an effective method at least during the breeding season. This approach will give a relatively good indication of seasonal abundance and distribution of birds on the installation, but not as complete a picture as the effort described in (1) above.

3. **Two-season Surveys**. If 4-season surveys are not possible, efforts should be focused on the breeding and wintering seasons, with techniques similar to that described in (2) above. This will provide the best possible coverage for SOC on installations during times where bird communities are seasonally established and do not include transient migrants.

4. **Breeding-season Surveys**. If only a one-season survey is possible, that effort should typically be focused during the breeding season, with surveys conducted as widely as possible throughout the installation. Breeding birds will be vocal and will have established territories. Area searches or, perhaps, point-counts (similar to 2 above) are best suited to identify SOC and other species during this season.

If Species of Concern are detected during the baseline survey, installations may choose to develop specific monitoring programs for them. Since bird populations are changing constantly, DoD may also wish to repeat the entire baseline survey every 5-10 years. These additional surveys will also assist in supporting an installations INRMP.

Where SOC or significant concentrations of migratory birds are found a decision will have to be made about whether the numbers are large enough, and the likelihood of effects due to military activities is likely enough, that monitoring is warranted under the Migratory Bird MOU. This analysis will provide much of the information needed to decide what level of accuracy is needed in the monitoring and how to design the surveys to achieve the target accuracy. A few brief guidelines for design of these surveys can be offered, however.

If military activities are deemed unlikely to affect the species, but sufficient doubt remains to trigger the "may effect" clause in the MOU, then monitoring probably can be infrequent and rapid methods probably can be used. For example, if a landbird SOC breeds in a training area where few impacts on the bird are expected, but a decision is made to monitor its populations, then a few quick surveys while birds are establishing territories (and are easy to survey) and perhaps an assessment of reproductive success (e.g., nest-monitoring, late season mist-netting) may be appropriate. If direct, substantial effects are likely to occur, then more intensive methods may be needed. This was the case on Farallon de Medinilla (FDM), an island located approximately 150 miles north of Guam in the Pacific Ocean. FDM is an important island for both military training and nesting seabirds. The DoD has used FDM target ranges since 1976, and the island is an important nesting site for more than a dozen species of migratory seabirds. Conservationists expressed concern about effects of the training on the seabirds. A protracted legal battle followed. Monthly aerial surveys were initiated in 1997 and continue to the present time. They show that, since 1997, there have been no clear changes in the numbers of most species, and one species has increased (Vogt, unpub. data, 2008). This example clearly shows the value of obtaining monitoring data when military activities may affect species of concern.

On installations or parts of installations that are accessible to the public, one or both of the initial surveys described above might be augmented, or even replaced, by encouraging participation in the eBird program. This program permits easy recording of birds detected using various survey methods and the data, if collected by members of the public, would not cost DoD anything to obtain. Tens of thousands of observations from throughout the U.S. and beyond are recorded monthly through the eBird program. Recording data from installations in eBird has the advantage that assessing status near to—as well as on—the installations may be possible.

Given large sample sizes, it has proven possible to detect large changes in abundance across space or time with eBird (although the program is too new to have undergone formal, independent review in the refereed literature). Records entered in eBird usually are not selected randomly under a well-defined sampling plan so estimating density or population size is usually not possible, but trends in density may be more important to estimate. A particularly powerful approach would be to use eBird for initial identification of SOC and then to use designed surveys to monitor their status. The data collected from designed surveys, however, also should be entered in eBird both to support that program and to facilitate comparisons of populations on and off the installation. For more information on eBird, visit *www.ebird.org*.

Chapter 8: Recommendations for Participation in Large-Scale Surveys

As noted throughout this report, DoD has been a major supporter of avian monitoring, especially through its Legacy and SERDP programs. In the past, however, there was not a DoD-wide policy statement about the extent and kind of participation by DoD in regional and larger-scale monitoring programs. The bird monitoring MOU signed by NABCI members (table 1), the MOU with the USFWS (table 2), and the Migratory Bird Rule (table 3), all make it clear that DoD is a significant partner in and contributor to large-scale bird monitoring programs. Furthermore, the value of such programs is clear. Most management issues, in fact, are regional in scope and thus require regional-level data. This Chapter suggests ways for DoD to participate in regional and larger scale programs.

The following criteria can be used to determine the level of DoD participation in large-scale surveys: (1) if the lands to be surveyed are under DoD management and are very important to the focal species, then greater participation by DoD will have a greater benefits for both the resource and to DoD; (2) if the lands to be surveyed are not under DoD management, but are still very important to the focal species (e.g., on migration or wintering areas), then greater participation by DoD also will have greater benefits for both the resource and DoD. These guidelines are illustrated below by discussing appropriate DoD participation in the BBS and the MAPS program.

Breeding Bird Survey

The BBS is a well-established, widely-endorsed, long-term survey that provides some of the best evidence on the status of birds in North America (Sauer and others, 1997). Many BBS routes on DoD installations are surveyed by volunteers. DoD could help the survey the most—and could serve its own interests best—by encouraging coverage of routes that are on or near to its installations with installation personnel and partnerships with volunteers. Many such routes exist (table 10). For example, 30 routes that cross at least one DoD installation were surveyed on fewer than half of the years between 1995 and 2004 and the same was true of 109 routes that were within 10 km of one or more installations. The BBS office has indicated (Keith Pardieck, personal communications, February 2010) that they would be pleased to work with DoD on a plan for identifying those routes that are not surveyed regularly.

Table 10. Number of Breeding Bird Survey (BBS) routes classified by distance to a DoD installation and recent survey frequency.

Minimum distance (km) between installation and BBS route	Number of routes surveyed 1995–2004 during	
	0–4 years	5–10 years
0	30	150
5	82	568
10	109	854
25	210	1,718

Monitoring Avian Productivity and Survival (MAPS)

The MAPS monitoring protocol is a standardized breeding season mist-netting and banding protocol that is currently used by more than 450 monitoring stations continent-wide. The MAPS program (DeSante, 1999; DeSante and others, 2005a; Saracco and others, 2008) is more complex, and perhaps less well known, than the BBS so it is described in some detail below. Following the description, we suggest how the criteria above might be used to determine DoD's participation in this survey. Readers interested in learning more about the MAPS Program should contact The Institute for Bird Populations (IBP).

Since 1994, DoD has supported the operation of 135 MAPS landbird demographic monitoring stations on military lands (for one or more years) and the development of landbird management guidelines and management decision support tools. Overall, 99 stations were operated by IBP in one or more years. By 2007, a network of 58 long-term MAPS stations existed on 11 installations, strategically placed to monitor the demographics of landbird populations in the context of military mission-oriented land management.

Since 1994, the DoD Legacy Resource Management Program, Army Corps of Engineers, and Naval Facilities Engineering Command have provided logistical support and annual funding for:

a. The operation of MAPS stations on (or associated with) 22 military installations, of which 78 operated in any year between 1994 and 2002. Since 2003, 48 of those 78 stations were operated annually plus another 10 stations that were added to the network. This has resulted in more than 104,500 bird captures of 77,500 individual birds and 168 species, of which 23 species were captured >1,200 times.

b. Reorganization of the original monitoring network (78 stations) to better focus on species of conservation concern (since 2002). By 2007, 58 stations were active on 11 installations organized to monitor the management of species of conservation concern in response to land-management activities associated with Readiness and Range Sustainment (Nott and others, 2007, table 11). Clusters of stations were located in several Bird Conservation Regions: Central Hardwoods (24), Texas Oaks and Prairies (12), Edwards Plateau (6), Southeastern Coastal Plain (6), Appalachian Mountains (4), and Atlantic Northern Forest (6).

c. Calculation of landbird demographic variables (e.g., survival, productivity, population trend, body condition) from proofed and verified banding data (1994–2007).

d. Reporting of the results of demographic analyses to individual installations (or groups of installations) and the DoD Legacy Resource Management Program.

e. Construction of landscape-scale ecological models in which demographic variables for 10 species of conservation concern were used as response variables to landscape metrics derived from the National Land Cover Dataset (Nott and others, 2003).

f. Development of measures of population health or performance using a suite of demographic (and landscape) "performance measures" that allow managers to compare the within-installation demographic status of landbird populations with the status of populations in the surrounding region (Nott and others, 2007).

g. The formulation of species management guidelines and development of decision-support tools that help land managers predict the impact of alternate management scenarios on the demographic performance of multiple species of concern.

h. Analyses that have identified important relationships between avian demographics and a suite of spatio-temporal climate and weather variables. This is critical information to managers because the effects of weather and climate on environmental conditions, and in turn, on bird populations, must be accounted for when assessing the efficacy of management on landbird population demographics.

In addition, 38 MAPS stations operated independently of IBP on 23 DoD installations. However, only 20 of these stations were still operational in 2007. Data collected from these independent stations were analyzed to determine their efficacy in monitoring species of conservation concern (Nott and others, 2005). All publications relating to MAPS monitoring of landbird populations on military lands can be accessed through IBP's website.

Two additional programs from IBP contribute valuable demographic data during the non-breeding season to DoD managers. These winter monitoring projects include the MoSI (Monitoreo de Sobrevivencia Invernal) program across the northern Neotropics and the MAWS (Monitoring Avian Winter Survival) program in temperate North America. MoSI is designed to address monitoring, research, and management goals. The monitoring goal of MoSI is to provide estimates of monthly, overwintering, and annual survival rates and indices of late winter physical condition for a suite of 25 landbird species for various habitats and geographic regions.

Research goals of MoSI include:
- the statistical modeling of survival and physical condition as functions of age, sex, habitat, geographic location, and weather,
- linking winter population parameters with breeding season vital rates and population trends, and
- the development of predictive population models.

Management goals of MoSI are to
- use research results to develop strategies for reversing population declines and maintaining healthy populations, and
- evaluate management actions through an adaptive management framework.

Like MAPS, MoSI relies on the establishment of a geographically extensive network of mist-netting and banding stations to meet program goals. MoSI cooperators also contribute feather samples to the Center for Tropical Ecology at UCLA for molecular analyses aimed at linking breeding and wintering populations. The MAWS program was initiated in 2003 as a 4-year pilot project on four southeastern U.S. military installations. MAWS shares goals and protocols with MoSI but targets short-distance migrants and species that are year-round residents of temperate North America. In addition to the MAWS stations operated on military installations, several independent MAWS station operators have contributed data to the MAWS program.

As the material above indicates, MAPS is a well-established, widely endorsed large-scale survey. It has been specifically mentioned in various documents (see tables 1–3) as one of the surveys that DoD should support. MAPS stations are not located using a random sampling plan so an analysis, based on proximity of MAPS stations to DoD installation, like that carried out above for the BBS routes, could not be undertaken. DoD's participation in MAPS should be determined primarily by the extent to which the areas surveyed by MAPS stations will provide important information about the *populations* of concern, regardless of whether they are on DoD land. DoD thus may choose to participate in MAPS programs where their support will do the most good, even if this is far from DoD installations. Indeed, monitoring efforts on DoD installations may be most

Table 11. Current DoD-MAPS monitoring objectives relating to Readiness and Range Sustainment identifying DoD locations (number of MAPS stations) and target species (including two USFWS Focal Species—Wood Thrush and Painted Bunting).

[This work was funded by the DoD Legacy Resource Management Program (Project Number 00103). Scientific bird names in alphabetical order by common name: Acadian Flycatcher (*Empidonax virescens*), Blue-winged Warbler (*Vermivora pinus*), Cerulean Warbler (*Dendroica cerulean*), Field Sparrow (*Spizella pusilla*), Kentucky Warbler (*Oporornis formosus*), Louisiana Waterthrush (*Seiurus motacilla*), Painted Bunting (*Passerina ciris*), Prairie Warbler (*Dendroica discolor*), Red-cockaded Woodpecker (*Picoides borealis*), Wood Thrush (*Hylocichla mustelina*), Worm-eating Warbler (*Helmitheros vermivorum*)]

Installation	State	Monitoring objectives and target species
Fort Bragg (6)	NC	Effects of fire regimes intended to prevent wildfire and manage for Red-cockaded Woodpecker (USFWS Endangered Species status) on Prairie Warbler populations.
Jefferson Proving Ground (6)	IN	Effects of fire regimes and buffer forest thinning on populations of four forest species (Acadian Flycatcher, Wood Thrush, Worm-eating Warbler, Kentucky Warbler) and three successional species (Blue-winged Warbler, Prairie Warbler, and Field Sparrow).
Fort Knox (6)	KY	All monitored species in decline (including Wood Thrush). Effectiveness monitoring of powerline corridor management targeting Blue-winged Warbler
NWSC Crane (6)	IN	Effects of forest management relating to weapons storage on five forest species (Acadian Flycatcher, Wood Thrush, Worm-eating Warbler, Louisiana Waterthrush, and Kentucky Warbler) and three successional species(Blue-winged Warbler, Prairie Warbler, and Field Sparrow).
Fort Leonard Wood (6)	MO	Effects of forest management and fire regimes intended to reduce fuel loads and create fire breaks on five forest species and three successional species (same species as NWSC Crane). Also conduct annual Cerulean Warbler surveys.
Fort Hood (6)	TX	Monitoring of three successional species (including Painted Bunting) with intent to manage oak-prairie habitats for military drop zone using prescribed fire regimes.
Camp Bowie (6)	TX	Monitoring of three successional species (including Painted Bunting) under installation-wide restoration efforts including fire and cessation of cattle grazing (2007) intended to open TXARNG training areas.
Camp Swift (6)	TX	Effects of fire and habitat alteration used to manage military drop zone activities on performance measures of Painted Bunting populations.

effective if coupled with comparable monitoring efforts outside of installations (e.g., MAPS stations in the landscapes surrounding installations), or even during migration or on the Neotropical wintering grounds of SOC to DoD (e.g., as in the Monitoreo de Sobrevivencia Invernal [MoSI] program; DeSante and others, 2005b).

Chapter 9: Implementation

Implementation needs to be guided by DoD personnel. The NABCI Opportunities for Improving Avian Monitoring report (U.S. NABCI Monitoring Subcommittee, 2007), the Northeast Bird Monitoring Handbook (Lambert and others, 2009), this CBM Plan, and the subsequent implementation strategy provide guidance that DoD personnel may find helpful in implementing successful monitoring programs. Substantial work also will be needed to explain and refine the procedures for designing short-term projects (Chapter 4), selecting field methods (Chapter 5), and placing the data in appropriate repositories (Chapter 6). A proposal to do this work has been submitted to the DoD Legacy Program and was funded in 2009 and 2010. It includes the following description of the approach to be used:

The CBM Plan provides comprehensive guidance on how to design, conduct, and document bird monitoring programs and store the resulting data in national and international, password-protected, databases. Implementation of the CBM Plan will help insure that DoD carries out its responsibilities for bird monitoring under various federal rules and agreements, and that monitoring is conducted as efficiently as possible (e.g., that avian monitoring projects have a well-defined management focus and limited monitoring funds are placed where they will have most benefit to DoD). Although these changes are needed and will help DoD discharge its obligations to migratory birds, while at the same time saving money, implementation will not necessarily occur quickly or easily. In particular, DoD biologists will need assistance and encouragement in (a) design of monitoring programs including documentation, (b) selection of specific field methods to be used, (c) analysis of results, (d) preparation of metadata, and (e) submission of the data collected to data repositories. This project to help DoD implement the CBM Plan will provide extensive technical assistance on tasks (a)-(e) above.

A Team consisting of both USGS and DoD personnel will identify installations considering or already carrying out bird monitoring programs and will work with natural resources managers to implement the CBM Plan, especially steps (a)-(e) above. We expect to work with approximately 15-20 installations per year and that assistance will average about one person-week per installation, though the time needed will likely vary considerably depending on the scope and complexity of the project(s) on which our assistance is needed. DoD personnel (especially Rich Fischer and Chris Eberly with whom we have been working closely on the CBM Plan) have agreed to provide the initial contacts and will explain the procedures in the CBM Plan to installation biologists. USGS staff to be hired for this project, along with the PI, Jonathan Bart (whose salary is covered as a contribution from USGS), will provide advice as needed especially about design, choice of field methods, and analysis. The USGS personnel will take the lead in helping installation biologists prepare metadata and format the data they collect for entry into the Coordinated Bird Monitoring Database at the USGS offices in Boise, Idaho. Annual reports will be submitted each year summarizing the assistance provided and discussing how DoD biologists are assuming responsibility for the planning of future monitoring efforts. Based on this work revisions will be made to the CBM Plan as needed. For example, our intention is to add the most comprehensive and relevant monitoring program descriptions to the Plan as examples for other natural resources managers to follow. American Bird Conservancy will also be engaged in assisting with the completion of a comprehensive implementation plan document.

In addition, carrying out the implementation strategy described above will ensure that the DoD CBM Plan is reviewed and revised where necessary and that it is implemented throughout DoD.

Acknowledgments

We thank the following contributors for preparing sections of this report: Dr. Andrew Farnsworth of the Cornell Laboratory of Ornithology, for information on acoustics and telemetry; Dr. Sidney Gauthreaux, Clemson University Radar Ornithology Laboratory, information on radar technology; Dr. Peter Marra, Smithsonian Migratory Bird Center, for information on stable isotopes, and Drs. Phil Nott and David DeSante, Institute for Bird Populations, for information on Monitoring Avian Productivity and Survivorship. Report review was provided by members of the Department of Defense Partners in Flight Working Group. These individuals included Drs. Michael Guilfoyle (U.S. Army ERDC) and Eric L. Kershner (Marine Corps Base Camp Pendleton, CA); Messrs. Jeff Bolsinger (Fort Drum, NY), Gene Augustine (Remote Air Force Sites, Alaska), Greg Fleming (Fort Belvoir, VA), Matt Klope (NAVFAC BASH Coordinator, WA), John Arnett (Luke AFB, AZ), John Joyce (NAES Lakehurst, NJ), Jay Rubinoff (Army Environmental Command, MD), Dana Bradshaw (Fort Lee, VA), Jeff Keating (Fort Riley, KS), Tim Burr (PIF Representative, Emeritus); Ms. Michael Farrell Wright (NAS Oceana, VA) and Ms. Carol Finley (Kirtland AFB, NM).

References Cited

American Bird Conservancy and National Audubon Society, 2007, WatchList 2007, available at *http://www.abcbirds.org/abcprograms/science/watchlist/index.html*.

Bart, J., 2005, Guidelines for designing short-term bird monitoring programs, *in* Ralph, C.J., and Rich, T.D., eds., Bird Conservation Implementation and Integration in the Americas: Proceedings of the Third International Partners in Flight Conference, March 20-24, 2002: Asilomar, California, v. 2: General Technical Report, PSW-GTR-191, U.S. Department of Agriculture, Forest Service, p. 985-992.

DeSante, D.F., 1999, Patterns of productivity and survivorship from the MAPS program, *in* Bonney, R., Pashley, D.N., Cooper, R.J., and Niles, L., eds., Strategies for Bird Conservation: The Partners in Flight Planning Process, Cornell Laboratory of Ornithology.

DeSante, D.F., Nott, M.P., and Kaschube, D.R., 2005a, Monitoring, modeling, and management: why base avian management on vital rates and how should it be done?, *in* Ralph, C.J., and Rich, T.D., eds., Bird Conservation Implementation and Integration in the Americas: Proceedings of the Third International Partners in Flight Conference, March 20-24, 2002: Asilomar, California, v. 2: General Technical Report, PSW-GTR-191, U.S. Department of Agriculture, Forest Service, p. 795-804.

DeSante, D.F., Sillett, T.S., Siegel, R.B., Saracco, J.F., Romo de Vivar Alvarez, C.A., Morales, S., Cerezo, A., Kaschube, D.R., Grosselet, M., and Mila, B., 2005b, MoSI (Monitoreo de Sobrevivencia Invernal): Assessing habitat-specific overwintering survival of Neotropical migratory landbirds, *in* Ralph, C.J., and Rich, T.D., eds., Bird Conservation Implementation and Integration in the Americas: Proceedings of the Third International Partners in Flight Conference, March 20-24, 2002: Asilomar, California, v. 2: General Technical Report, PSW-GTR-191, U.S. Department of Agriculture, Forest Service, p. 926-936.

Department of Defense, 2006, Memorandum of understanding between the U.S. Department of Defense and the U.S. Fish and Wildlife Service to promote the conservation of migratory birds: Federal Register, v. 71, no. 168, August 30, 2006.

Farnsworth A., Gauthreaux, S.A., Jr., and Blaricom, D., 2004, A comparison of nocturnal call counts of migrating birds and reflectivity measurements on Doppler radar: Journal of Avian Biology, v. 35, p. 365-369.

Guilfoyle, M.P., and Fischer, R.A., 2007, Implementing Avian Inventory and Monitoring Efforts on Corps of Engineers Project Lands. EMRRP Technical Notes Collection (ERDC TN- EMRRP-SI-32), U.S. Army Engineer Research and Development Center: Vicksburg, Mississippi, *http://el.erdc.usace.army.mil/publications.cfm?Topic=technote&Code=emrrp.*

Igl, L.D., 1996, Bird checklists of the United States: Jamestown, North Dakota, Northern Prairie Wildlife Research Center Online: *http://www.npwrc.usgs.gov/resource/birds/chekbird/index.htm* (Version 12MAY2003).

Lambert, J.D., Hodgman, T.P., Laurent, E.J., Brewer, G.L., Iliff, M.J., and Dettmers, R., 2009, The Northeast Bird Monitoring Handbook. American Bird Conservancy: The Plains, Virginia, 32 p., Available online at *http://www.nebirdmonitor.org/handbook/nehandbook.*

Northeast Coordinated Bird Monitoring Partnership, 2007, A Framework for Coordinated Bird Monitoring in the Northeast: Northeast Coordinated Bird Monitoring Partnership Report, p. 62, Available online at *http://www.nebirdmonitor.org/framework.*

Nott, M.P., DeSante, D.F., and Michel, N., 2003, Management Strategies for Reversing Declines in Landbirds of Conservation Concern on Military Installations: A Landscape-scale Analysis of MAPS data: A report to the Legacy Resources Management Office, Washington. D.C.

Nott, M.P., DeSante, D.F., Pyle, P., and Michel, N., 2005, Managing Landbird Populations in Forests of the Pacific Northwest Region: The Institute for Bird Populations, no. 254.

Nott, M.P., and Morris T., 2007, Performance Measure Analysis: Examples of Comparing and Contrasting Installation-Specific Demographics with Regional Demographics and Landscape Characteristics: Point Reyes Station, California, Technical Report to the U.S. Department of Defense Legacy Resources Management Program, Contribution, no. 324 of The Institute for Bird Populations.

Oakley, K., Thomas, L.P., and Fancy, S.G., 2003, Guidelines for long-term monitoring protocols: Wildlife Society Bulletin, v. 31, p. 1000-1003.

Ridgely, R.S., Allnutt, T.F., Brooks, T., McNicol, D.K., Mehlman, D.W., Young, B.E., and Zook, J.R., 2007, Digital Distribution Maps of the Birds of the Western Hemisphere, version 3.0., NatureServe: Arlington, Virginia.

Saracco, J.F., DeSante, D.F., and Kaschube, D.R., 2008, Assessing landbird monitoring programs and demographic causes of population trends. Journal of Wildlife Management, v. 72, p. 1665–1673.

Sauer, J.R., Hines, J.E., Gough, G., Thomas, I., and Peterjohn, B.G., 1997, The North American Breeding Bird Survey Results and Analysis: Version 96.4. Patuxent Wildlife Research Center: Laurel, Maryland.

U.S. Fish and Wildlife Service, 2007, Migratory bird permits; take of migratory birds by the Armed Forces: Federal Register, v. 72, no. 39, February 28, 2007.

U.S. NABCI Committee, 2007. Memorandum of Understanding Between all members of the U.S North American Bird Conservation Initiative Committee to adopt the goals, recommendations, and action items stated in the 2007 report of the NABCI Monitoring Sub-Committee, "Opportunities for Improving Avian Monitoring". Available on-line at *http://www.nabci-us.org/*.

U.S. NABCI Monitoring Subcommittee, 2007, Opportunities for improving avian monitoring: U.S. North American Bird Conservation Initiative Report, 50 p. Available from the Division of Migratory Bird Management, U.S. Fish and Wildlife Service, Arlington, VA; on-line at *http://www.nabci-us.org/aboutnabci/monitoringreportfinal0307.pdf*

Appendix A. List of Avian Studies at DoD Installations

Bird monitoring and assessment that we were able to learn about are listed on the following pages. We know, as several reviewers pointed out, that many other programs exist, but we could only include the ones that the official contacts at each installation identified for us.

State	Service	Installation Name	Study
AK	AF	Fort Yukon LRRS (611 CES)	None
AK	AF	Murphy Dome LRRS (611 CES)	None
AK	AF	Indian Mountain LRRS (611 CES)	None
AK	AF	Tatalina LRRS (611 CES)	BBS
AK	AF	Sparrevohn LRRS (611 CES)	None
AK	AF	Tin City LRRS (611 CES)	Kittlitz's Murrelet study Sandhill Crane migration/windpower
AK	AF	Cape Lisburne LRRS (611 CES)	Eider study Kittlitz's Murrelet study
AK	AF	Kotzebue LRRS (611 CES)	Eider study
AK	AF	Point Barrow LRRS (611 CES)	Eider study Eider migration Raven nest chronology Breeding biology of Steller's eiders nesting near Barrow, AK
AK	AF	Oliktok LRRS (611 CES)	Eider study Brant study
AK	AF	Barter Island LRRS (Kaktovik) (611 CES)	Eider study
AK	AF	Cape Romanzof LRRS (611 CES)	Kittlitz's Murrelet study BASH survey Nesting biology and population ecology of yellow wagtails Avifaunal inventory
AK	AF	Cape Newenham LRRS (611 CES)	Kittlitz's Murrelet study Periodic Wildlife Surveys
AK	AF	Cold Bay LRRS (611 CES)	Included in USFWS BBS route
AK	AF	Bullen Point SRRS (611 CES)	Eider study
AK	AF	Wainwright SRRS (611 CES)	Eider study
AK	AF	Point Lay former LRRS (611 CES)	Eider study
AK	AF	Point Lonely former SRRS (611 CES)	Eider study
AK	AF	Clear Air Force Station	
AK	AF	Eareckson Air Station	Winter wildlife surveys Harlequin Duck diet contamination study Point count monitoring BASH surveys Spring & Fall Wildlife Surveys CBC Goose Forage Study
AK	AF	Eielson Air Force Base	Waterfowl brood and geese surveys BASH monitoring

State	Service	Installation Name	Study
AK	AF	Elmendorf Air Force Base	Monitoring Bird Migrations and Movements with Radar and Landsat Imagery-II Bohemian waxwing monitoring Alaska Loon Watch Owl monitoring Point count monitoring Raptor nesting habitat
AK	Army	Black Rapids Training Area	None
AK	Army	Donnelly Training Area	Alaska Landbird Monitoring Survey Cavity nesting ducks box project Sharp-tailed grouse lek surveys Whimbrel nest site survey Ruffed grouse survey
AK	Army	Fort Greely	None
AK	Army	Fort Richardson	INRMP Avian Projects BBS CBC
AK	Army	Fort Wainwright	Boreal owl nest box project
AK	Army	Gerstle River Training Area	None
AK	Army	Tanana Flats Training Area	Owl monitoring Swan nesting and brood survey
AK	Army	Yukon Training Area	Alaska Landbird Monitoring Survey Cavity nesting duck box project Ruffed grouse survey Owl monitoring
AK	Army/NG	Stewart River Training Area - National Guard	Breeding bird survey (different from national program)
AL	AF	Maxwell Air Force Base	
AL	Army	Anniston Army Depot	Survey of Breeding Birds
AL	Army	Fort Rucker	None
AL	Army	Redstone Arsenal	None (breeding bird study planned for 2007)
AL	Army/NG	Fort McClellan - National Guard	Point count survey
AL	Navy	OLFs - Whiting Field	
AR	AF	Little Rock Air Force Base	4-season point count landbird surveys
AR	Army	Pine Bluff Arsenal	
AR	Army/NG	Camp J.T. Robinson - National Guard	Nearctic-Neotropical Migrants pt cts (years) Bachman's Sparrow survey Loggerhead Shrike Survey Brown-headed Cowbird Survey Northern Bobwhite Survey Cerulean Warbler Survey
AR	Army/NG	Fort Chaffee - National Guard	Annual Bird Count MAPS / MAWS Greater Prairie Chicken search
AZ	AF	Davis-Monthan Air Force Base	Migratory linkages of Burrowing Owls Dispersal Patterns of Burrowing Owls on Davis-Monthan AFB
AZ	AF	Luke Air Force Base	

State	Service	Installation Name	Study
AZ	AF/MC	Barry M. Goldwater Range	Migratory linkages of Burrowing Owls
AZ	Army	Fort Huachuca	Grassland Bird Transect Monitoring Hummingbird Monitoring Mexican Spotted Owl Monitoring Southwestern Willow Flycatcher and Yellow-billed Cuckoo Surveys Wintering Ecology of Shrubland Birds
AZ	Army	Yuma Proving Ground	Migratory linkages of Burrowing Owls Wintering Ecology of Shrubland Birds Use of wildlife water developments by birds during migration
AZ	Army/NG	Camp Navajo - National Guard	Songbird monitoring
AZ	Army/NG	Florence Military Reservation - National Guard	
AZ	MC	MCAS Yuma	Migratory linkages of Burrowing Owls Wintering Ecology of Shrubland Birds
AZ	Navy	Flagstaff, NAVOBSY	None
CA	AF	Beale Air Force Base	Waterfowl Use of Wetland and Upland Nesting Habitats Surveys for Special-Status Aquatic Invertebrate, Botanical, and Wildlife Resources Hunting and Nesting Success of the Northern Harrier in Yellow Star-thistle Utility Pole Use and Electrocutions of Raptors Breeding bird point count survey (2005)
CA	AF	Edwards Air Force Base	Migratory linkages of Burrowing Owls Bird study at Edwards AFB Wintering Ecology of Shrubland Birds
CA	AF	March Joint Air Reserve Base	Migratory linkages of Burrowing Owls Burrowing Owl Monitoring at March Reserve Base
CA	AF	McClellan Air Force Base	
CA	AF	Travis Air Force Base	None
CA	AF	Vandenberg Air Force Base	SW Willow Flycatcher Study
CA	Army	Camp Parks (Reserve Forces Training Area)	
CA	Army	Fort Hunter Liggett	
CA	Army	Fort Irwin	Migratory linkages of Burrowing Owls Wintering Ecology of Shrubland Birds
CA	Army	Presidio of Monterey	None
CA	Army	Sierra Army Depot	None (several in past)
CA	Army/NG	Camp Roberts - National Guard	Bald eagle monitoring on the Nacimiento River MAPS
CA	Army/NG	Camp San Luis Obispo - National Guard	CBC
CA	Army/NG	Van Vleck Training Area - National Guard	

State	Service	Installation Name	Study
CA	MC	Marine Corps MWTC Bridgeport	Riparian Bird Monitoring and Habitat Assessment in the Upper East and West Walker River Watersheds
CA	MC	MCAGCC Twentynine Palms	Burrowing Owls
CA	MC	MCAS Miramar	California Gnatcatcher Surveys Southwestern willow flycatcher and least Bell's vireo surveys MAPS
CA	MC	MCB Camp Pendleton	Migratory linkages of Burrowing Owls
CA	MC	MCLB Barstow	Riparian Bird Survey on the Mojave River
CA	MC	MCRD San Diego	
CA	Navy	China Lake, NAWS	Migratory linkages of Burrowing Owls Wintering Ecology of Shrubland Birds BASH Bird use survey
CA	Navy	Chocolate Mountains Gunnery Range	
CA	Navy	Concord Detachment, NWS Seal Beach	
CA	Navy	Coronado, NAB	Migratory linkages of Burrowing Owls NAS North Island and Naval Outlying Field Imperial Beach BASH Project, Bird Survey and Data Collection CA Least Tern and Snowy Plover Monitoring Burrowing Owl Monitoring San Diego Bay Waterbird Surveys
CA	Navy	Dixon Navy Radio Transmitter Facility	
CA	Navy	El Centro, NAF and Ranges	Migratory linkages of Burrowing Owls
CA	Navy	Fallbrook Detachment, NWS Seal Beach	Migratory linkages of Burrowing Owls
CA	Navy	Imperial Beach, NOLF (inset)	
CA	Navy	Lemoore, NAS	Migratory linkages of Burrowing Owls An Adaptive Management Plan for the Burrowing Owls at NAS Lemoore
CA	Navy	Monterey, NPS	
CA	Navy	Mountain Warfare Training Ctr, La Posta	
CA	Navy	Naval Radio Receiving Facility Imperial Beach (inset)	
CA	Navy	North Island, NAS (inset)	CBC
CA	Navy	Point Loma, Naval Base (inset)	
CA	Navy	Point Mugu, NAS	T & E surveys Monthly surveys for shorebirds, waders, raptors and some passerines
CA	Navy	Port Hueneme, CBC	Brown pelican count
CA	Navy	San Clemente Island, NALF	San Clemente Island Loggerhead Shrike
CA	Navy	San Diego, NAVSTA (inset)	
CA	Navy	San Nicolas Island, NOLF	

State	Service	Installation Name	Study
CA	Navy	Seal Beach, NWS	Migratory linkages of Burrowing Owls
CA	Navy	Warner Springs, SERE Camp	
CO	AF	Buckley Air Force Base	Migratory linkages of Burrowing Owls Burrowing Owl surveys
CO	AF	Peterson Air Force Base	none
CO	AF	Schriever Air Force Base	Migratory linkages of Burrowing Owls
CO	AF	US Air Force Academy	Breeding Bird Census
CO	Army	Fort Carson	Migratory linkages of Burrowing Owls
CO	Army	Piñon Canyon Maneuver Site	Migratory linkages of Burrowing Owls
CO	Army	Pueblo Chemical Depot	Monitoring Colorado's Birds
CO	Army/FWS	Rocky Mountain Arsenal National Wildlife Refuge	Migratory linkages of Burrowing Owls
CO	Navy	Navy Oil Shale Reserve	
CT	Army/NG	Nehantic Training Site	
CT	Navy	New London, NSB	
CU	Navy	Naval Base Guantanamo Bay	
DE	AF	Dover Air Force Base	Migratory Bird Monitoring using Automated Acoustic and Internet Technologies
FL	AF	Avon Park AFR	Species at risk monitoring Bald eagle nest survey
FL	AF	Cape Canaveral Air Force Station	Seasonal bird surveys via installation-wide point counts Florida Scrub-Jay monitoring (yearly) Shorebird survey BASH point counts
FL	AF	Eglin Air Force Base	Red-cockaded woodpecker Shorebird surveys and nest monitoring Bald eagle monitoring Southeastern American Kestrel nesting Cavity nester community with RCW Longleaf pine restoration monitoring Habitat use by neotropical migrants Fall migration monitoring via radar/ground-based transects
FL	AF	Homestead Joint Air Reserve Base	
FL	AF	MacDill Air Force Base	None
FL	AF	Patrick Air Force Base	Seasonal bird surveys via installation-wide point counts Least Tern nesting surveys Shorebird survey BASH point counts
FL	AF	Tyndall Air Force Base	International Piping Plover Census
FL	Army	Malabar Transmitter Annex	Seasonal bird surveys via installation-wide point counts
FL	Army/NG	Camp Blanding - National Guard	Red-cockaded woodpecker Wild turkey Bald eagle
FL	Navy	Jacksonville, NAS	Neotropical migratory bird study

State	Service	Installation Name	Study
FL	Navy	Key West, NAS	Least tem nest monitoring Bald eagle nest monitoring
FL	Navy	Mayport, NAVSTA	Neotropical Migrant checklist survey International Shorebird Survey
FL	Navy	Navy Coastal Systems Station (Panama City)	
FL	Navy	NOLF Whitehouse	Neotropical migratory bird study
FL	Navy	OLFs - Whiting Field	Neotropical migratory bird study
FL	Navy	Pensacola, NAS	
FL	Navy	Pinecastle Impact Range	
FL	Navy	Rodman Bomb Target	
FL	Navy	Stevens Lake Bombing Range	
FL	Navy	Whiting Field, NAS	
GA	AF	Dobbins Joint Air Reserve Base	
GA	AF	Moody AFB + Grand Bay Range	BASH point counts
GA	AF	Robins Air Force Base	
GA	Army	Fort Benning	RCW monitoring MAWS LCTA survey
GA	Army	Fort Gillem	
GA	Army	Fort Gordon	
GA	Army	Fort McPherson	
GA	Army	Fort Stewart	Wood duck nest box monitoring Bobwhite quail cock count Swallow-tailed kite monitoring Red-cockaded woodpecker conservation and recovery
GA	Army	Hunter Army Airfield	
GA	Army/NG	Catoosa Range Training Site	
GA	MC	MCLB Albany	
GA	MC	Townsend Range	
GA	Navy	Kings Bay, NSB	
HI	AF	Bellows Air Force Station	
HI	AF	Hickam Air Force Base	
HI	Army	Kahuku Training Area/ Army Training Range	
HI	Army	Pohakuloa Training Area	
HI	Army	Schofield Barracks Military Reservation	
HI	MC	Marine Corps Base Hawaii, Kaneohe Bay	
HI	Navy	Barking Sands, PMRF	Laysan Albatross Egg Relocation Project Wedge-tailed Shearwater Monitoring Shorebird surveys
HI	Navy	Kaula Rock	
HI	Navy	Lualualei, NAVMAG	Point counts for endangered species Point counts for all species Elepaio playback surveys Endangered waterbird survey at Niuli'I Ponds

State	Service	Installation Name	Study
HI	Navy	NCTAMS Pacific Wahiawa	Flora and fauna survey
HI	Navy	Pearl Harbor, NAVSTA	
IA	Army	Iowa Army Ammunition Plant	
IA	Army/NG	Camp Dodge - National Guard	Avian species catalogue Avian and predator habitat use profiles in an agricultural matrix Avian communities on two prairie pothole wetlands Borrow area wetland mitigation monitoring
ID	AF	Juniper Butte Range	Raptor nest searching
ID	AF	Mountain Home AFB	Area search all species Sage grouse lek surveys Hummingbird banding
ID	AF	Saylor Creek Air Force Range	
ID	Army/NG	Kimama Training Area - National Guard	
ID	Army/NG	Orchard Training Area - (Idaho) National Guard	
ID	Navy	Bayview Det., Carderock NSWC	
IL	AF	Scott Air Force Base	Breeding bird survey via pt cts Spring migration survey Winter birds survey (all done in 2001)
IL	Army	Joliet Training Area	Long-term ecological study
IL	Army	Rock Island Arsenal	None
IL	Army/FWS	Lost Mound NWR (Savanna Army Depot)	
IL	Army/FWS	Midewin National Tallgrass Prairie (Joliet Arsenal)	
IL	Army/NG	Marseilles Training Area - National Guard	
IL	Navy	Great Lakes, NTC	
IN	AF	Grissom Joint Air Reserve Base	
IN	Army	Indiana Army Ammunition Plant	
IN	Army	Kingsbury Training Area	
IN	Army	Newport Chemical Depot	
IN	Army/FWS	Big Oaks NWR (Jefferson Proving Ground)	
IN	Army/NG	Camp Atterbury - National Guard	Surveys of State listed species CBC
IN	Navy	Crane, NSA	Indiana Breeding Bird Atlas MAPS in past T& E survey 2005
KS	AF	Forbes Field	
KS	AF	McConnell Air Force Base	
KS	AF	Smoky Hill Air Force Range	BBS Effects of management regimes on breeding bird densities
KS	Army	Fort Leavenworth	CBC MAPS in past

State	Service	Installation Name	Study
KS	Army	Fort Riley	Auditory Quail Survey Bald Eagle Diurnal Habitat Utilization Henslow's Sparrow Line Transects and Point Counts Bald Eagle Nocturnal Roost Utilization Prairie-Chicken Lek Survey Ring-necked Pheasant Survey Kansas Shorebird Surveys Winter Raptor Survey
KS	Army	Kansas Army Ammunition Plant (Parsons)	BBS Riparian species nest success and diversity
KY	Army	Blue Grass Army Depot (North and South polygons)	
KY	Army	Fort Campbell	
KY	Army	Fort Knox	PIF Point Counts (summer and winter 2005- installation wide surveys)
KY	Army/NG	Artemus Training Site - National Guard	
KY	Army/NG	Wendell Ford Regional Training Center - Nat. Guard	
LA	AF	Barksdale Air Force Base	Observational Wild Turkey Survey
LA	Army	Fort Polk	MAPS Winter abundance of and habitat use by Henslow's Sparrows Spring and fall migration monitoring via radar/ground-based transects (2005-06) CBC Raptor migration study Eastern bluebird monitoring Point count monitoring of residents and neotropical migrants Kestrel nest box study
LA	Army/NG	Camp Beauregard -National Guard	
LA	Army/NG	Camp Minden - National Guard	
LA	Army/NG	Camp Villere - National Guard	
LA	Navy	New Orleans, NAS JRB	
MA	AF	Hanscom Air Force Base	
MA	AF	Westover Air Reserve Base	
MA	AF/Army/NG	Massachusetts Mil. Res. (Otis ANGB/Camp Edwards)	
MA	Army	Fort Devens (Reserve Forces Training Area)	
MD	AF	Andrews Air Force Base	None
MD	Army	Aberdeen Proving Ground	Maryland Breeding Bird Atlas Bald eagle investigations
MD	Army	Fort Detrick	
MD	Army	Fort George G. Meade	
MD	Army	Fort Ritchie	

State	Service	Installation Name	Study
MD	Army/NG	Baker Training Site (Lil Aaron Strauss) - Nat. Guard	
MD	Navy	Annapolis USNA	
MD	Navy	Bloodsworth Island	
MD	Navy	Carderock, NSWC	None
MD	Navy	Indian Head, NSWC	Bald eagle monitoring
MD	Navy	Patuxent River, NAS	MAPS Nest box monitoring Migratory Bird Monitoring using Automated Acoustic and Internet Technologies
ME	AF/FWS	Aroostook NWR (Loring AFB)	
ME	Army/NG	Bog Brook/Riley Training Site - National Guard	
ME	Army/NG	Caswell Training Site - National Guard	
ME	Army/NG	Deepwoods Training Site - National Guard	
ME	Navy	Brunswick, NAS	
ME	Navy	Navy SERE Facility (Rangeley, Redington)	
ME	Navy	NCTAMS Cutler	
MI	AF	Selfridge Air Guard Base	
MI	Army/NG	Camp Grayling - National Guard	
MI	Army/NG	Fort Custer Training Center - National Guard	Raptor inventory Edge effects on avian nest predator Reproductive success, brood parasitism, and nest predation of forest-nesting neotropical migrants
MN	Army/NG	Arden Hills Training Site	
MN	Army/NG	Camp Ripley - National Guard	Bald eagle monitoring Ruffed grouse and wild turkey survey Red-shouldered hawk survey Bluebird nest box monitoring CBC Owl survey Annual songbird surveys Yellow rail monitoring
MO	AF	Whiteman Air Force Base	Point counts
MO	Army	Fort Leonard Wood	Spring migrant survey Great Blue Heron colony survey MAPS
MO	Army	Lake City Army Ammunition Plant	
MO	Army/NG	Camp Clark - National Guard	
MO	Army/NG	Camp Crowder Training Site - National Guard	
MO	Army/NG	Macon Training Site - National Guard	

Appendix A. List of Avian Studies at DoD Installations.—Continued

State	Service	Installation Name	Study
MO	Army/NG	Wappapello Training Site - National Guard	Bald eagle nest survey CBC Bluebird and wood duck nest box monitoring
MO	Army/NG	Weldon Spring Training Site - National Guard	
MS	AF	Columbus Air Force Base	Wildlife hazard assessment Endangered and threatened species survey
MS	AF	Keesler Air Force Base	
MS	Army	Mississippi Army Ammo Plant	
MS	Army/NG	Camp McCain - National Guard	
MS	Army/NG	Camp Shelby - National Guard	
MS	Navy	Gulfport, NCBC	
MS	Navy	Meridian, NAS	None
MS	Navy	Multi-Purpose Target Range	None
MS	Navy	NOLF Joe Williams	None
MS	Navy	Pascagoula, NAVSTA	
MS	Navy	Searay Target Range	None
MT	AF	Malmstrom Air Force Base	None
MT	Army/NG	Bearmouth Training Area - National Guard	
MT	Army/NG	Fort William H. Harrison - National Guard	
MT	Army/NG	Limestone Hills Training Center - National Guard	
NC	AF	Dare County Range	
NC	AF	Pope Air Force Base	
NC	AF	Seymour Johnson Air Force Base	BASH point counts
NC	Army	Camp Mackall	Red-cockaded woodpecker monitoring
NC	Army	Fort Bragg	Investigation of the American Kestrel MAPS, MAWS (MoSI) Red-cockaded woodpecker monitoring Grassland Bird Surveys (2000)
NC	Army	Military Ocean Terminal Sunny Point	Red-cockaded woodpecker monitoring CBC
NC	Army/NG	Camp Butner - National Guard	
NC	MC	Atlantic Outlying Field	
NC	MC	Bogue Field	
NC	MC	MCAS Cherry Point	Point count monitoring Effects of aircraft activities on waterfowl at Piney Island RCW baseline survey
NC	MC	MCAS New River	
NC	MC	MCB Camp Lejeune	Red-cockaded woodpecker (many studies) International Piping Plover Census State aerial waterfowl survey In past – Painted bunting study Other shorebird monitoring?

State	Service	Installation Name	Study
NC	MC	Piney Island (Point of Marsh Target)	
NC	Navy	Harvey Point, DTA	
NC	Navy	Oak Grove Holt Navy Airfield	
ND	AF	Grand Forks Air Force Base	Seasonal bird surveys via pt cts installation-wide (2001 and 2004) Migration monitoring via radar
ND	AF	Minot Air Force Base	
ND	Army/NG	Camp Grafton - National Guard	
ND	Army/NG	Camp Grafton South - National Guard	
ND	Army/NG	Garrison Training Area - National Guard	
NE	AF	Offutt Air Force Base	
NE	Army/NG	Camp Ashland - National Guard	
NE	Army/NG	Cushing Training Site - National Guard	
NE	Army/NG	Greenlief Training Site (Hastings) - National Guard	
NE	Army/NG	Mead Training Area - National Guard	
NE	Army/NG	Stanton Training Site - National Guard	
NH	AF	New Boston Air Force Station	Birds in forested landscapes Whippoorwill monitoring
NJ	AF	McGuire Air Force Base	None
NJ	AF	Warren Grove Gunnery Range	Point counts
NJ	Army	Fort Dix	Bald eagle nest and foraging survey NJ winter bald eagle surveys Grasshopper sparrow nesting Raptor surveys Spring bird counts
NJ	Army	Fort Monmouth	None
NJ	Army	Picatinny Arsenal	Hawk Watch Bluebird nest box monitoring Passerine anecdotal info recorded Migratory Bird Monitoring using Automated Acoustic and Internet Technologies
NJ	Navy	Earle, NWS	Wetland Mitigation Area Monitoring Report 2005
NJ	Navy	Lakehurst, NAES	Grassland Bird Survey Migratory Bird Monitoring using Automated Acoustic and Internet Technologies Forest Bird Survey Nest box and platform monitoring
NM	AF	Cannon Air Force Base	Migratory linkages of Burrowing Owls Endangered, Threatened, Candidate and Sensitive Bird Species

State	Service	Installation Name	Study
NM	AF	Holloman Air Force Base	Migratory linkages of Burrowing Owls Boles Wells Water System Annex Bird Surveys Wetland bird nesting and aquatic invertebrate occurrence
NM	AF	Kirtland Air Force Base	Migratory linkages of Burrowing Owls Population Status, Reproductive Success, Prey Availability, Site Fidelity and Migration of Western Burrowing Owls Grey vireo monitoring Loggerhead shrike monitoring MAPS starting 07 Long-term songbird monitoring 07
NM	AF	Melrose Air Force Range	Endangered, Threatened, Candidate and Sensitive Bird Species and Birds of Conservation Concern
NM	Army	Fort Bliss McGregor Range	Wintering Ecology of Shrubland Birds
NM	Army	Fort Wingate Depot Activity	
NM	Army	White Sands Missile Range	Wintering Ecology of Shrubland Birds Migratory linkages of Burrowing Owls Mexican Spotted Owl habitat evaluation Pinyon Jay monitoring Delineation of southwestern willow flycatcher and yellow-billed cuckoo habitat Seasonal landbird surveys in riparian/wetlands (1997-98)
NM	Army/NG	Black Mountain Training Site (Deming) - Nat. Guard	
NM	Army/NG	Camel Tracks Training Site - National Guard	
NM	Army/NG	Farmington Training Site - National Guard	
NM	Army/NG	Happy Valley Training Site (Carlsbad) - Nat. Guard	Threatened and Endangered Species Survey
NM	Army/NG	Roswell Training Site - National Guard	
NV	AF	Creech Air Force Base	
NV	AF	Nellis Air Force Base	Migratory linkages of Burrowing Owls
NV	AF	Nellis Air Force Range	
NV	Army	Hawthorne Army Depot	
NV	Army/NG	Henderson Training Site - National Guard	
NV	Army/NG	Stead Training Site - National Guard	
NV	Navy	Fallon Training Range Complex	None

State	Service	Installation Name	Study
NV	Navy	Fallon, NAS	Nevada Breeding Bird Atlas Aquatic Bird Survey Monthly point counts CBC BASH Spring Wings
NY	Army	Fort Drum	Migratory Bird Monitoring using Automated Acoustic and Internet Technologies
NY	Army	West Point Military Reservation	Migratory Bird Monitoring using Automated Acoustic and Internet Technologies Spatial Distribution and Habitat Associations of Cerulean Warblers
OH	AF	Wright-Patterson Air Force Base	
OH	Army/NG	Newton Falls Training Site (NG)	
OK	AF	Altus Air Force Base	None
OK	AF	Tinker Air Force Base	Bird Inventory and Migration Trends
OK	AF	Vance Air Force Base / Kegelman Auxiliary Airfield	
OK	Army	Fort Sill	MAPS Black-capped Vireo Study
OK	Army	Lexington Army Aviation Facility	
OK	Army	McAlester Army Ammunition Plant	None
OK	Army/NG	Camp Gruber - National Guard	
OR	AF	West Coast Over the Horizon Backscatter Radar Sys.	
OR	Army	Umatilla Chemical Depot	
OR	Army/NG	Biak Training Center - National Guard	
OR	Army/NG	Camp Adair - National Guard	
OR	Army/NG	Camp Rilea - National Guard	
OR	Army/NG	Camp Withycombe - National Guard	
OR	Navy	Boardman, NWSTF	Migratory linkages of Burrowing Owls
PA	Army	Carlisle Barracks	
PA	Army	Letterkenny Army Depot	
PA	Army	New Cumberland Army Depot	
PA	Army	Tobyhanna Army Depot	
PA	Army/NG	Beaver Dam Training Site - National Guard	
PA	Army/NG	Fort Indiantown Gap - National Guard	Raptor Population Index Project Nest Box Monitoring Abundance and Diversity of Breeding Birds 2nd PA Breeding Bird Atlas Summer / winter owls and northern goshawk surveys eBird, opportunistic bird surveys Waterbird monitoring

State	Service	Installation Name	Study
PA	Army/NG	Marshburg Training Area - National Guard	
PA	Navy	Willow Grove, NAS JRB	
SC	AF	Charleston Air Force Base	
SC	AF	Poinsett Range (Shaw AFB)	RCW monitoring MAPS Raptor survey Northern bobwhite survey
SC	AF	Shaw Air Force Base	Least Tern monitoring BASH
SC	Army	Fort Jackson	MAPS Red-cockaded woodpecker monitoring Southeastern American Kestrel and Wood Duck nest box monitoring
SC	Army/NG	Leesburg Training Site (McCrady TC) -National Guard	
SC	MC	MCAS Beaufort	Migratory bird monitoring
SC	MC	MCRD Parris Island	
SC	Navy	Charleston, NWS	Point counts
SD	AF	Ellsworth Air Force Base	Burrowing owl use of prairie dog towns
TN	AF	Arnold Air Force Base	Bald Eagle Status and Distribution Heron Monitoring MAPS Henslow's Sparrow Monitoring Nightjar Monitoring
TN	Army	Holston Army Ammunition Plant	Bird checklist
TN	Army	Milan Army Ammunition Plant	BBS
TN	Army/NG	Volunteer Training Site-Milan - National Guard	
TN	Army/NG	Volunteer Training Site-Smyrna - National Guard	
TN	Army/NG	Volunteer Training Site-Tullahoma - National Guard	
TN	Navy	Mid-South, Naval Support Activity (Memphis)	
TX	AF	Brooks City-Base	None
TX	AF	Dyess Air Force Base	Spring point counts Bluebird nest box monitoring CBC Riparian restoration area- long-term monitoring of avian response
TX	AF	Goodfellow Air Force Base	
TX	AF	Kelly Annex (Lackland AFB)	
TX	AF	Lackland Air Force Base	
TX	AF	Laughlin Air Force Base	
TX	AF	Randolf Air Force Base	Golden-cheeked warbler habitat
TX	AF	Sheppard Air Force Base	Migratory bird surveys
TX	Army	Camp Bullis	Endangered species survey (long-term monitoring of GCWA and BCVI) All bird checklist
TX	Army	Fort Bliss	Migratory linkages of Burrowing Owls

State	Service	Installation Name	Study
TX	Army	Fort Hood	Endangered species monitoring Genetic Differentiation in the Endangered Black-Capped Vireo MAPS
TX	Army	Fort Sam Houston	
TX	Army	Lonestar Army Ammo Plant	
TX	Army	Longhorn Army Ammo Plant	
TX	Army	Red River Army Depot	
TX	Army/NG	Camp Bowie - National Guard	MAPS Black-capped vireo habitat survey Annual black-capped vireo survey
TX	Army/NG	Camp Maxey- National Guard	Baseline survey of birds
TX	Army/NG	Camp Mabry – National Guard	Bird species diversity & abundance Plant species on bird transects
TX	Army/NG	Camp Swift - National Guard	MAPS Avian richness and abundance Vegetation survey at bird sample points
TX	Army/NG	Fort Wolters - National Guard	Inventory of birds
TX	Navy	Corpus Christi, NAS	BASH International Piping Plover Grassland Bird Survey USGS
TX	Navy	Escondido Ranch (McMullen Range, Dixie Target)	Grassland Bird Survey USGS
TX	Navy	Ft Worth, NAS JRB	
TX	Navy	Ingleside, NAVSTA	
TX	Navy	Kingsville, NAS	BASH Grassland Bird Survey USGS
TX	Navy	NALF Orange Grove	BASH Grassland Bird Survey USGS
UT	AF	Hill Air Force Base	Bird Risk Assessment Population, Distribution and Habitat Study for Threatened, Endangered and Sensitive Species
UT	AF	Hill Air Force Range (Utah Test & Training Range)	Population Monitoring of Neotropical Migratory Birds BBS
UT	AF	Wendover Air Force Auxillary Field	
UT	AF	Wendover Range	
UT	Army	Deseret Test Center	BASH Nest boxes
UT	Army	Dugway Proving Ground	Raptor banding Eagle monitoring MAPS Nest boxes Hawkwatch
UT	Army	Tooele Army Depot (2 polygons)	None
UT	Army/NG	Camp Williams - National Guard	
VA	AF	Langley Air Force Base (inset)	
VA	Army	Craney Island Disposal Area (inset)	

State	Service	Installation Name	Study
VA	Army	Fort AP Hill	MAPS Nest box monitoring
VA	Army	Fort Belvoir	Multi-season avian surveys via installation-wide point counts BASH point counts CBC BBS Bluebird nest box Shorebird survey Chimney swift roost survey Waterfowl survey Bald Eagle nest surveys Wild Turkey roost and winter track counts
VA	Army	Fort Eustis (inset)	Breeding Bird Survey (1999) Spring Migration Survey (2000)
VA	Army	Fort Lee	Breeding Bird point counts Biological Surveys and Inventories Nest box program CBC Wading bird surveys
VA	Army	Fort Monroe (inset)	
VA	Army	Fort Story (inset)	Breeding Bird Survey (1999) Spring Migration Survey (2000)
VA	Army	Radford Army Ammunition Plant	CBC Sporadic surveys
VA	Army/NG	Camp Pendleton State Mil. Res. - Nat. Guard (inset)	
VA	Army/NG	Fort Pickett - National Guard	
VA	MC	Marine Corps Base Quantico	MAPS
VA	Navy	Camp Peary	
VA	Navy	Craney Island Fuel Depot (inset)	
VA	Navy	Dahlgren, NSF	Bluebird Nest Boxes Eagle nest surveys In past – MAPS and point counts
VA	Navy	Dam Neck Annex (inset)	
VA	Navy	Fentress, NALF	MAPS (in past) BASH
VA	Navy	Little Creek, NAB (inset)	MAPS (in past)
VA	Navy	Norfolk, Naval Base (inset)	MAPS (in past) BASH
VA	Navy	Norfolk, Naval Shipyard (inset)	
VA	Navy	Norfolk-Northwest Annex, NSA	MAPS (in past)
VA	Navy	Oceana, NAS (inset)	MAPS (in past) BASH
VA	Navy	St. Julian Creek Annex (inset)	
VA	Navy	Yorktown, NWS	Northern bobwhite count Mute swan and Canada goose counts
VT	Army/NG	Camp Johnson - National Guard	
VT	Army/NG	Ethan Allen Firing Range - National Guard	

State	Service	Installation Name	Study
WA	AF	Fairchild Air Force Base	Survey of birds and mammals RTHA survey planned
WA	AF	McChord Air Force Base	Range-wide Streaked Horned Lark Assessment MAPS, Nest box monitoring
WA	AF	McChord Training Annex	
WA	AF/USFS	Cusick Survival Training Site	
WA	Army	Fort Lewis	Range-wide Streaked Horned Lark Assessment MAPS Nest box and cavity monitoring RTLA bird surveys
WA	Army	Yakima Training Center	Sage grouse lek surveys
WA	Army/NG	Camp Bonneville	
WA	Army/NG	Camp Murray	None
WA	Army/USFS	Mount Baker Helicopter Training Area (3 polygons)	
WA	Army/USFS	Nap of the Earth Helicopter Training Area	
WA	Navy	Everett, NAVSTA	
WA	Navy	Indian Island, NAVMAG	
WA	Navy	Jim Creek, NAVRADSTA (T)	
WA	Navy	Kitsap, Naval Base	CBC
WA	Navy	Puget Sound, Naval Shipyard	
WA	Navy	Whidbey Island, NAS	NOHA and BAEG surveys
WA	Navy	NSB Bangor	CBC
WI	AF	Hardwood Range (Volk Field)	
WI	AF	Volk Field (ANGB)	
WI	Army	Badger Army Ammunition Plant	
WI	Army	Fort McCoy	Eagle and osprey monitoring Distribution, abundance and productivity of grassland birds Winter finch banding Ruffed grouse drumming survey
WI	Army/NG	Camp Wismer - National Guard	
WV	Army/NG	Camp Dawson - National Guard	
WV	Navy	Sugar Grove, NIOC	MAPS
WY	AF	F.E. Warren Air Force Base	Survey for breeding birds on Crow Creek (pt cts) Mountain Plover surveys Mountain Plover habitat
WY	Army/NG	Camp Guernsey - National Guard	
WY	Army/NG	Lander Training Area - National Guard	
WY	Army/NG	Lovell Training Area - National Guard	
WY	Army/NG	Sheridan Training Area - National Guard	
WY	Navy	Navy Petroleum Reserve	

www.ingramcontent.com/pod-product-compliance
Lightning Source LLC
Chambersburg PA
CBHW080433290526
45791CB00008BA/2486